THE ULTIMATE COERCIVE SANCTION: A CROSS-CULTURAL STUDY OF CAPITAL PUNISHMENT

Keith F. Otterbein

HRAF PRESS
New Haven, Connecticut
1986

ABOUT THE AUTHOR:

Keith F. Otterbein is Professor of Anthropology, at the State University of New York at Buffalo. His Ph.D. in Anthropology was received in 1963 from the University of Pittsburgh. He has done field work on Andros and Abaco Islands in the Bahamas and in the Mandara Mountains of Northeast Nigeria. His published works include *The Evolution of War* (1970/85–2nd Edition 1985) and numerous journal articles on his primary interests, which include political anthropology (law and war), social structure (family organization), as well as cross-cultural research and ethnographic research methods.

Cover Design: Marylou Finch.

INTERNATIONAL STANDARD BOOK NUMBER: 0-87536-346-6
LIBRARY OF CONGRESS CATALOG CARD NUMBER: 86-80163
© COPYRIGHT 1986
HUMAN RELATIONS AREA FILES, INC.
NEW HAVEN, CONNECTICUT
ALL RIGHTS RESERVED
PRINTED IN THE UNITED STATES OF AMERICA

Acknowledgments

This has been the most difficult cross-cultural study I have conducted. Throughout the research I was forced to proceed inductively, rather than deductively (see Chapter 3). This meant that at most steps of the way I did not have well-formulated theories and hypotheses to guide me. Furthermore, the ethnographic materials that form the heart of the research were unpleasant reading in nearly all instances. The only enjoyable case was that of the condemned man who escaped from the island of Tikopia, rather than commit "judicial suicide" (see Chapter 1, pp. 5–6, and Chapter 9, footnote 1, pp. 118–119). Moreover, the controversial nature of capital punishment in the United States has led some acquaintances to raise questions concerning my politics, my motivations, and even my personality structure. Those desiring more specific answers to their questions than the thoughts provided in the Prologue, Chapters 1 to 3, and the Epilogue will have to ask me.

Many individuals have helped me in different ways to complete this arduous study. My wife, Charlotte Swanson Otterbein, has aided in many more ways than can be mentioned. Just a few include theoretical discussions, statistical advice, computer analyses, editing, and corrections using a word processor. If the study were on a different topic, I would dedicate this book to her. My son, Gere Frederic Otterbein, has indirectly encouraged the study through his interest in capital punishment; in his reading he found a reference to William Jones' death, and, I believe, correctly interpreted it as a case of capital punishment (see Chapter 1, pp. 4–5). Friend and neighbor James Sedwick on occasion provided newspaper clippings dealing with current debates and executions. Miriam Norris typed the manuscript on the departmental word processor. Librarian Marilyn Haas frequently assisted with the locating of sources. Another librarian, Charles D'Aniello, prepared the index. Students who helped on specific tasks are acknowledged at appropriate points. Anthropological colleagues with whom I have discussed capital punishment include Barton Brown, Charles Clark, Melvin Ember, Celia Ehrlich, Patrick Gray, Susan Horan, and A. T. Steegmann, Jr. Colleagues outside of anthropology with whom I have discussed the study include economist Isaac Ehrlich, sociologist Simon Singer, and psychologists Ronald Gentile and Robert Nichols. Special thanks goes to the Law School at the State University of New York at Buffalo, where I spent my sabbatical leave (1979–1980); Dean Thomas Headrick gave his permission to audit courses and Associate Dean Barry Boyer helped in arranging my schedule. Credit must be given to the members of HRAF's pubilcation committee, in particular to HRAF President Robert O. Lagacé, for being willing to publish a study which explores a topic previously not subjected to cross-cultural analysis. Elizabeth Swift copyedited the manuscript. And finally, mention should be made of my graduate school mentor at the University of Pittsburgh, the late George Peter Murdock. I have paid him honor–the kind of honor I believe he would have appreciated—by including at two points information highly critical of two of his nemises.

Acknowledgments for Permissions

Acknowledgment is gratefully made to the following publishers for permission to reprint:

AMERICAN MUSEUM OF NATURAL HISTORY, for:

Excerpt from "Death by Decree: An Anthropological Approach to Capital Punishment," *Natural History* 87 (5), 50–67, 1978, page 55. Reprinted by permission of American Museum of Natural History.

AMERICAN PUBLIC HEALTH ASSOCIATION, for:

Excerpt from "Anthropology and Its Contribution to Public Health," by George P. Murdock, *American Journal of Public Health* 42: 7–11, 1952. Reprinted by permission of The American Public Health Association.

CBS COLLEGE PUBLISHING, for:

Excerpt from *The Dobe !Kung*, by Richard B. Lee, copyright © 1984 by CBS College Publishing, pp. 95–96. Reprinted by permission of CBS College Publishing.

COLUMBIA UNIVERSITY PRESS, for:

Excerpt from *The Concept of Cultural Systems: A Key to Understanding Tribes and Nations*, by Leslie A. White, 1975, page 32. Reprinted by permission of Columbia University Press.

DOUBLEDAY AND COMPANY, INC. for:

Excerpt from *Wayward Servants: The Two Worlds of the African Pygmies,* by Colin Turnbull, copyright © 1965 by Colin M. Turnbull, page 190. Reprinted by permission of Doubleday & Company, Inc.

EDINBURGH UNIVERSITY PRESS, for:

Excerpt from *Custom, Law, and Terrorist Violence,* by Edmond Leach, pp. 31–32, 1977. Reprinted by permission of Edinburgh University Press.

JAI PRESS, INC. for:

Excerpt from "Notes Toward a Theory of Punishment and Social Change," by Steven Spitzer, *Research in Law and Sociology* 2: 207–229, 1979, pages 209–210. Reprinted by permission of JAI Press, Inc.

JOURNAL OF ANTHROPOLOGICAL RESEARCH, for:

Excerpt fom "Higi Armed Combat," by Keith F. Otterbein, *Southwestern Journal of Anthropology* 24: 195–213 (1968), page 203. Reprinted by permission of Journal of Anthropological Research.

NAPOLEON A. CHAGNON, for:

Excerpt from "Is Reproductive Success Equal in Egalitarian Societies?" *Evolutionary Biology and Human Social Behavior: An Anthropological Perspective,* edited by N. A. Chagnon and William Irons, pp. 374–401, 1979, page 394. Reprinted by permission of Napoleon A. Chagnon.

Contents

List of Tables

Prologue

The major conclusion of this study is that capital punishment is a cross-cultural universal: all cultures or societies utilize the penalty of death, from time to time, to dispose of individuals who have commited acts that are felt by members of the group to be harmful or threatening to them and to their society. Whether this result is seen as surprising or not, an extensive literature review begun in 1975 has revealed no publication in which the universality of capital punishment has been either hypothesized or obtained as a finding by a social scientist. In this study, the data base for arriving at the conclusion that capital punishment is characteristic of all cultures has been a 60-society probability sample taken from the Human Relations Area Files. Of the 51 societies for which there were sufficient data, all 51 societies use the death penalty. A nonsystematic attempt to discover societies outside the sample that do not have capital punishment has produced no examples, but rather has produced evidence of capital punishment in some unanticipated cases.

The death penalty is an element that transforms some customs and mores into laws. The most widely used definition of law employs three elements: official authority, regularity, and privileged force (Hoebel 1954: 28, Otterbein 1977: 134). The death penalty is the most extreme form of privileged force, or physical coercion; it is the ultimate coercive sanction.[1] Therefore, it is a central, integral part of every legal and political system; it has been institutionalized by all cultures. Capital punishment holds this keystone role because it is the most effective means of physical coercion that political leaders as well as community members have available for disposing of criminals whose continued existence is threatening to the community. Because of the fundamental importance of capital punishment in all legal and political systems, political leaders try to arrogate to themselves the right to execute. In general, the more complex the political system, the more successful these leaders have been. In the simplest cultures, those without councils, but with strong, localized kinship groups, political leaders are unable to claim effectively the privilege of using the death penalty. In these cultures, the right to execute lies with the kinship group. In complex cultures, political leaders are often, but not always, able with the aid of councils and supporters to arrogate to themselves the right to execute. The efforts of political leaders in different types of political systems to control the use of the death penalty have created modifications in the nature of capital punishment.

This study has found that capital punishment is what anthropologists have called a "cross-cultural universal" or "universal culture trait." The fact that it is universally found does not mean that executions are frequent occurrences in most cultures. Although the death penalty is always present among the cultural practices available to political leaders for dealing with threats to individuals and to the community, its universal availability does not lead to frequent use of capital punishment in most societies. And although ethnographic data do not permit the calculation or estimation of the frequency of occurrence of capital punishment, in terms of population size and/or time, the data strongly suggest that, in most cultures, the use of the death penalty is an infrequent occurrence, reserved for dealing with only those situations that are seen as severe threats to the community's existence. These situations vary, as does the legal process associated with capital punishment. An analysis of the variations in the manner in which capital punishment has been institutionalized in societies at different levels of political complexity constitutes a major portion of this study.

CHAPTER 1

Capital Punishment as a Topic of Social Science Investigation

Anthropologists, as well as other social scientists, have been little concerned with the study of capital punishment. A literature search initiated in 1975 and continued to the present has revealed a paucity of materials. Existing sources are found largely in the criminal justice area, and most of them deal with the effect of capital punishment as a deterrent (Miller 1980). In contrast to studies of deterrence, this cross-cultural study deals primarily with the causes of capital punishment and the various forms it takes in human society. Why have social scientists not been interested in studying capital punishment? Three reasons suggest themselves.[1]

First, executions have seldom been witnessed by anthropologists or others who were engaged in field research. Unlike many of the cultural practices that are observed frequently in a field situation, capital punishment is not a phenomenon that forces itself upon the attention of anthropologists. It is not a practice that is a part of a normal life cycle—such as birth and marriage—nor is it a practice that is a part of a normal annual cycle—such as planting and harvesting; indeed, by its very nature, capital punishment is a practice that comes into use only in response to circumstances that deviate from the normal. With the exception of despotic states, capital punishment is typically an infrequent occurrence; in some cultures, the circumstances under which it comes into play may tend to keep it from the attention of anthropologists, even if they are in the community. If executions are not witnessed, and if the field researcher is unaware that they occur, there is nothing for the ethnographer to explain.

One anthropologist who has witnessed an execution is Colin Turnbull (1978: 62), but this execution occurred in the United States rather than among the Pgymies of the Congo, who have been extensively studied by Turnbull (1965). Another anthropologist, William Jones, apparently witnessed his own "execution." He was killed by Ilongots, in the northern Philippines, on April 3, 1909, as he was attempting to leave their territory, with an extensive ethnographic collection, after nearly a year of fieldwork among these people. Although the Philippine government treated his killing as a murder and convicted three Ilongots for his death (they later escaped), the incident appears to be capital punishment from an Ilongot point of view. Jones repeatedly demanded bamboo rafts (balsas) from the Ilongot to transport his artifacts. When six rafts were not provided, he held a headman hostage. Jones' last diary entry on April 2 reads (Stoner 1971: 12–13):

> Then I told him [Takadan, a headman] to send runners through his district and bring me six balsas and six men by tomorrow forenoon; that if the balsas were not here I would take him down the river with me. He tried to persuade me to let him go home and urge his people to comply with my wants, but I told him he had lied to me so often that I could not believe him any longer. I told him to go sit down and not leave the house until I gave him permission to do so and to send anyone he wished to carry messages to his people. Tolan was in calling distance and he went off in the rain and gathering darkness with what I had told Takadan.

The next day Jones and his two servants were approached by Ilongots who promised rafts. Jones was struck by a bolo on the neck, slashed across the arm, and stabbed with a spear below the heart. Although the three men fought off the Ilongot and escaped by boat, Jones died later in the day (Stoner 1971: 13). Since Jones had detained and threatened a headman, his killing the next day appears to have been both planned and sanctioned by the Ilongots. The circumstances surrounding his "execution" appear to meet the three elements used to define capital punishment (see Chapter 2).

Only three first-hand descriptions occur in the ethnographic literature for the 60-society sample used in this study. One is Malinowski's account of a self-inflicted execution by a Trobriand Islander (see Chapter 4, pp. 24–25). The other is Speke's account of how the king of Ganda personally executed a woman with a rifle while Speke, a nineteenth-century explorer, was approaching the king's entourage (see Chapter 8, p. 81). He also saw women being led to execution. A line drawing is provided with the following passage (Speke 1864: 337–338):

> . . . nearly every day since I have changed my residence [to within the court precincts], incredible as it may appear to be, I have seen one, two, or three of the wretched palace women led away to execution, tied by the hand, and dragged along by one of the body-guard, crying out, as she went to premature death, "Hai minage!" (Oh my lord!) "Kbakka!" (My king!) "Hai n'yawo!" (My mother!) at the top of her voice, in the utmost despair and lamentation; and yet there was not a soul who dared lift hand to save any of them, though many might be heard privately commenting on their beauty.

A third account, which can also be considered first-hand, is W. H. R. Rivers' interview with a Tikopian who had escaped the death penalty by refraining from chopping a hole in the bottom of his canoe, a culturally prescribed practice. The man was fortunate in surviving, since Tikopia is a small, isolated Polynesian island, unlisted in many atlases. In Rivers' words (1914: 306):

> For severe offences the penalty is death, occasionally by hanging or possibly strangling, but more commonly by sending the offender out to sea; if a man, in a canoe; if a woman, by making her swim from the shore. The chief offence for which men are sent away is that already mentioned in which a man of the ordinary people is discovered in an intrigue with the daughter of a chief, and John could give no other example of an offence which involved this punishment. A man thus sent adrift is put at night in a canoe with some food which is provided by his father. The property of the victim— clubs, paddles, bows and arrows— is put in the canoe with him and he is decorated with armlets and a fillet of bark-cloth, such as is worn in dancing, is bound on his head. All this is done because it is recognized that the man is going to his death and, when the canoe has drifted out of the sight of land, the victim should take his club and break the bottom of the canoe so that he sinks and drowns. As the victim drifts away his relatives wail and

they follow the same rules of mourning as if the man had died a natural death on the island. When John was sent adrift he was given a mat-sail and having no wish to follow the orthodox Tikopian custom of dying when he had lost sight of land, he set sail and reached Vanikolo in three days, nourishing himself meantime on twelve coconuts which had been given him for food. Usually only two or three coconuts are given because it is understood that there will be no need for their use. The procedure in John's case differed from that customary in another respect in that he was sent off at midday instead of at night.

Eye-witness accounts of capital punishment do exist, however, in the ethnohistorical record. For example, Robert Heizer's "Executions by Stoning among the Sierra Miwok and Northern Paiute" gives verbatim accounts from several mid-nineteenth-century sources (1955). Moreover, just as ordinary citizens, we may witness on film (often seen on television) a variety of kinds of executions. Examples include the firing squad killing of Chinese and Cuban landowners by Communist revolutionaries, the shooting of ABC News correspondent Bill Stewart by soldiers at a government roadblock in Nicaragua in 1979 (better classified as a murder than as capital punishment), and artists' renderings on television newscasts of executions in the United States. Turnbull's article on capital punishment (1978) provides drawings by famed artist Ben Shahn. Once in a great while in traveling, a person has the misfortune to see an execution. A student at my university reported to me that she had witnessed two stonings in Iranian villages in the 1970s.

A second possible reason why social scientists have not studied capital punishment is that for nearly two hundred years the Western intellectual world has opposed capital punishment (Mackey 1982). Such opposition, in most instances, seems to have prevented Western intellectuals from studying the use of the death penalty. It is speculation on my part, but I think it is possible that they have avoided conducting any studies that might show the social functions of capital punishment. To show that the death penalty is functionally linked to other aspects of a social system could be construed as political support for capital punishment. In other words, researchers might be open to the charge that they are in favor of capital punishment; at the least they could be accused of providing "scientific" evidence that the pro-capital-punishment forces could use to advance their point of view. Although many organizations in the United States, such as the American Civil Liberties Union, oppose capital punishment (Bedau 1979; Schwarzschild 1982), approximately two-thirds of the American public favor capital punishment for premeditated murder (Stinchcombe et al. 1980: 28). Surveys done by the National Opinion Research Center (NORC) show that the number of people favoring the death penalty has increased from 57 percent in 1972 to 72 percent in 1980 (Davis 1980:81; calculations of percentages done by myself). With public support of this magnitude, it is not surprising that after a ten-year suspension of executions, the death penalty was reinstituted in the United States; on January 17, 1977, Gary Mark Gilmore was executed by firing squad in Utah. More executions followed: as of December 6, 1985, fifty executions have occurred.

A third possible reason why social scientists have not studied capital punishment is that, except for those scholars who have studied the despotic state (see Chapter 8), the role of capital punishment in society has not been viewed as important. While I have no evidence, I suspect that the failure to attribute importance to the use of the death penalty stems from the belief that capital punishment is not widely found in primitive societies. If a cultural practice is not common, it may be assumed to be unimportant. In my own case, I was unaware before the research was initiated that nearly all, if not all, societies have capital punishment. As a universal, it demands an explanation.

The above three reasons applied to my own situation. I have not witnessed an execution;[2] I was indifferent to capital punishment, either as a social problem or as a means of crime control; and I thought that it was unimportant as a topic for social science inquiry. Television viewing in the mid-1970s vividly brought to my attention the fact that Elizabethan England was a despotic state. The head of Mary, Queen of Scots, rolling on the floor is a sight that is readily remembered.[3] Thus I formulated the idea that capital punishment is a characteristic of state-level societies, for only at this level do political leaders have enough power to use executions to dispose of those who threaten their control of the apparatus of statehood. In the fall of 1980, with the assistance of several graduate students, I collected information from the Human Relations Area Files on several topics that pertain to political anthropology. One of these topics was capital punishment. Sufficient data were found to encourage me to initiate a cross-cultural study (see Chapter 3). Since completing this study, my views have changed. I now believe that capital punishment is an important topic for social science inquiry and that it is an important means of crime control.

Since social scientists have not systematically studied capital punishment, there was no developed body of theory to test, and there were no rival hypotheses. Thus the research strategy I employed consisted of fitting together "bits and pieces." The bits and pieces in most cases consisted of brief, one-paragraph discussions of capital punishment. Many of the sources for these brief discussions were published after 1975, as a perusal of the references will show. These pieces were arranged into three specific theories, each of which pertains to a different level of sociopolitical complexity. The levels are band, tribe, and chiefdom/state. The three theories show how political leaders and/or communities in each type of society cope with threats to individual or community well-being; the theories are developed in Chapters 6, 7, and 8. I have tested these theories, using cross-cultural research methodology (see Chapter 9). The ethnographic cases in the sample provide support for the theories. The verification of the theories, I believe, provides convincing evidence that capital punishment plays an important role in all societies. Thus capital punishment is a cultural practice that requires serious attention from social scientists. Discussion of this topic should not be relegated to debates, editorial columns, or cartoons.

CHAPTER 2

Capital Punishment Defined

Capital punishment may be defined as the "appropriate killing of a person who has committed a crime within a political community." It is closely related to several other forms of human violence: homicide, political assassination, feuding, warfare, and human sacrifice. In order to conduct comparative research, it was necessary to develolp a definition that would distinguish capital punishment from these other forms of killing. Only with such a precise definition is it possible to locate descriptions of capital punishment in the ethnographic literature and to set aside descriptions of related but different phenomena.

The definition of capital punishment offered above contains three elements: (1) The killing occurs within a political community or within a smaller unit of the political community. Generally, a political community is composed of local groups organized into a maximal territorial unit under the direction of a political leader (Otterbein 1977: 6–7, 122–127).[1] "Within" means that the execution takes place within a geographic area controlled by a political leader; although the person who is to be executed is likely to be a member of the political community, this is not necessarily the case—the person may belong to another political community. (2) The killing is defined as "appropriate" by the political leader or the leader of a subunit within the political community. Appropriate does not necessarily mean that the political leader or the leader of a smaller unit decides upon the execution or carries it out; it simply means that it has the approval of the leader. (3) There is a reason for the killing. Someone has performed an act (or a series of acts) that is considered to be a crime by the political leader or the leader of a subunit, and perhaps by some or all of the members of the political community. In other words, the person has done something that violates the norms or mores of the culture— he is a wrongdoer who has commited a crime and has thus threatened the well-being of the community. Not all crimes, of course, lead to capital punishment.

Capital punishment differs from the other related forms of killing. Homicide, political assassination, feuding, warfare, and human sacrifice are all defined by the presence of fewer than the three basic elements that define capital punishment. The following chart lists the elements that are present for each of these forms of human violence.

Homicide, political assassination, and feuding are all considered to be inappropriate by political leaders; this criterion differentiates them from capital punishment. However, like capital punishment, they occur within political communities. Homicide is the intentional or unintentional killing of another person. It takes place within a political community; that is, either the killer and his victim are both members of the same political community or else the political leader controls the region in which the killing has occurred. Political leaders do not approve or regard homicides as appropriate. Even the seeming exceptions to this statement— infanticide and euthanasia—are more likely to be condoned than approved. In most cultures, homicides, particularly intentional killings, are crimes.

Political assassination is the killing by a member (or members) of the political community of the political leader or of a person appointed by him; if the assassination is performed by someone who belongs to another political community, the act can be regarded as warfare. Political assassination is always disapproved, unless the political leader himself arranges to have a subordinate leader killed. Indeed, political assassination is usually itself labeled a crime.

Feuding is blood revenge following a homicide (Otterbein and Otterbein 1965: 1470). It is a counter-killing that takes place within the political community, which is not deemed appropriate by political leaders even though the reason for the killing is well understood by most members of the political community. (For an extensive discussion of the definition of feuding, see Boehm 1984 and Otterbein 1985.) On the chart, "Reason exists" is shown as being "present" in the case of feuding, because revenge of an injustice is an integral part of the definition of feuding. Like capital punishment, feuding is a response to a crime, the crime being a previous homicide.

Warfare is armed combat between political communities (Otterbein 1968c: 277); it is engaged in by the military organizations of two political communities (Otterbein 1970/85: 3–5). Since the killing occurs *between* political communities, rather than *within* them, the absence of this one element differentiates warfare from capital punishment. The other two elements are present: political leaders almost always regard going to war as an appropriate response to what they believe is an unjustifiable act perpetrated upon them. Capital punishment, however, may also occur during or after a war. Captives taken on the battlefield, members of the other political community who have been captured spying, or political and military leaders who surrender may all be subject to execution. Since the death penalty is administered within the political community, it is capital punishment, not warfare.

Human sacrifice is the most difficult of the related forms of killing to differentiate from capital punishment. Human sacrifice, like capital punishment, occurs within a political community and is deemed appropriate by political leaders. A recent cross-cultural study of human sacrifice defined it simply as a way to "approach the spirit world" and as an "institutionalized religious practice" (Sheils 1980: 245, 252). In other words, there is a culturally approved reason, supported by the political leaders and by the members of the political community, for killing the sacrificial victims. The persons who are offered to the deities have not necessarily committed crimes: they may be loyal subjects of a king or the wives and servants of a wealthy man. The Old Testament (Genesis 22) even gives an example of a father offering his son to a deity (who benignly interrupts the sacrificial procedure). Persons who have committed crimes or prisoners of war may also be used as sacrifices, however. When criminals and war captives—in other words, persons who have committed crimes—are used as sacrifices to the spirit world, the phenomenon can be classified as both capital punishment and human sacrifice. Thus, although capital punishment and human sacrifice are defined differently, certain practices described in ethnographic monographs can be classified as both. In this study, if the sacrificial victim is either a criminal or a war captive, the killing is deemed to be capital punishment.

Political communities with capital punishment are likely to have an explicit rule (a "law on the books") that executions constitute an appropriate response to certain crimes. However, capital punishment by definition does not require there to be an explicit rule present. On the other hand, a "law on the books" alone, never resulting in an execution, does not produce a political community with capital punishment. For capital punishment to exist, executions must occur on occasion. Furthermore, an explicit rule that there is no capital punishment cannot necessarily be accepted as evidence that there is no death penalty; if on occasion the law is set aside and an execution occurs, there is, of course, capital punishment (see Chapter 5, pp. 42–43 for examples). The recent creation of a "no capital punishment" law and/or the absence of capital punishment for a brief period is not sufficient reason to classify a political community as one without capital punishment. The United States for ten years had no executions (1967–1977). Should the United States have been classified as a country without capital punishment? No. The law was on the books and it was soon to be used again.

CHAPTER 3

Methodology

This study originated in an attempt to explain why political leaders execute and sometimes torture members of their own political community—and sometimes war captives as well. As I began this research in October 1975, I believed that capital punishment was found primarily at the state level of political complexity. I hypothesized that if political leaders feel threatened, severe punishment will be used to cope with the perceived threat; such a threat could be either internal (e.g., from assassins or traitors) or external (e.g., from spies or enemy agents). Over the next four years, I made little progress on the topic. A literature search, in part computer assisted, proved largely unproductive. Although capital punishment has been discussed by those working in judicial areas (Miller 1980), anthropologists and sociologists have seldom focused upon the topic. (The literature that was discovered is discussed in Part 3.) The paucity of sources, both theoretical and empirical, forced me to develop an inductive research strategy. In order to employ such an inductive strategy, a series of variables was developed, which deal with various aspects of capital punishment. These variables focused on the legal process that is related to capital punishment, on the execution itself, and on the reaction to the execution. (Each variable is described in detail in Chapter 4.) These were variables that could be used later to construct hypotheses and to test theories. If well-developed theories had already been present in the social sciences, I would have used a deductive strategy. From each rival theory, hypotheses would have been derived, and variables taken from these hypotheses would have been delineated. (For a step-by-step description of how to conduct a cross-cultural study, using a deductive research strategy, see Otterbein 1969a.)

The data base chosen for conducting the cross-cultural study of capital punishment is the Human Relations Area Files' (HRAF) Probability Sample Files (PSF). This is a stratified probability sample of 60 cultures, largely "primitive societies," which are contained within the larger group of approximately 325 cultures that make up the HRAF Files. The Probability Sample Files are described by Lagacé (1973); for technical discussions of how the PSF was constructed, see Otterbein (1976: 115–116) and Lagacé (1979); descriptions of each culture are to be found in *Sixty Cultures* (Lagacé 1977).[1] Each culture is a randomly chosen sampling unit from a geographical grouping of several well-described cultures. Thus the PSF is a representative sample of the world's best-described cultures. It is a worldwide sample of cultures, which range in size from small hunting and gathering bands to large states with complex economies. A major reason for choosing this sample over several other possible samples was its ready availability: a complete set of the HRAF Files is located in the Anthropology Department of the State University of New York at Buffalo.

Information found in the HRAF Files, including the PSF, is organized topically into numbered categories, using an "Outline of Cultural Materials" (Murdock et al. 1982). Two categories from this outline were selected that might deal with capital punishment. They are numbers 541 (spectacles) and 681 (sanctions). Without the guidance of the variables that had been developed for the study, three graduate students[2] gleaned passages from the ethnographic descriptions of the 60 cultures comprising the PSF (October 1980). Their only instruction was to record all instances of what they thought *might* be classified as capital punishment; they were told that if they had any doubts as to whether a cultural practice was or was not capital punishment, they should include the information. Information on 32 cultures was recorded. The amount of data was a clear indication that source material was available for conducting a cross-cultural study of capital punishment.

An inductive, comparative research method was employed, which used the Probability Sample Files (PSF) as its data base. The rationale for using an inductive approach in a cross-cultural study has been clearly explained by Maxwell and Maxwell (1980). In contrast to the deductive approach that I have recommended (Otterbein 1969a), they advocate "continuous comparative analysis." The essence of the method is that any data may be examined at any stage of the research; as the research progresses, concepts are formed, developed, and integrated into hypotheses. Specifically, this means that any culture that the researcher wishes to include in a cross-cultural study—on the basis either of being already familiar with it or of having discovered it during a literature review—may be incorporated into the data base; this procedure for gathering cases is called "theoretical sampling" by Maxwell and Maxwell. Each new case examined may lead to the modification and further development of the emerging hypothesis. Although my research was initiated before their recommendations were published (in November 1980), I have consciously used "continuous comparative analysis," examining cases that are not in the PSF as I developed my theories. However, I have not replaced probability sampling with theoretical sampling. Although I scrutinized any case that I believed might be relevant, there is a distinct advantage in adhering to probability sampling: The use of a stratified probability sample, such as the PSF, forces the researcher to consider cultures which might otherwise never have been examined. It also prevents the researcher from ignoring or discarding cases in the sample that do not easily fit into any of the emerging theories. To proceed as the Maxwells recommend could introduce bias into the sample. By using a probability sample, the researcher is able not only to make descriptive statements applicable to the sample but also to use inferential statistics.[3] The use of a probability sample that represents the world's best-described cultures permits the empirical testing of hypotheses that are intended to have universal application.

Ten variables were developed in the initial stage of the research into capital punishment; they reflect the various steps that may occur before, during, and after the death sentence has been carried out. The variables were arranged in this logical order on a code sheet (see Appendix A). Included with the capital punishment variables was a sheet of supplementary variables, which deal with a variety of important social and political dimensions. Using the code sheets, one for each culture, I coded or categorized data from the verbatim passages collected by the three students. Information on the sociopolitical variables was obtained either from these passages or from *Sixty Cultures*, HRAF's guide to the PSF (Lagacé 1977). As coding proceeded through the spring of 1981, a typology of political systems was developed. (The typology is described in detail in Chapter 9.) Each culture was classified as one of the eight political types that emerged.

As the coding and classification of cultures progressed, several more theoretical sources were discovered. These studies were specific to particular types of sociopolitical systems. At this point in the research, I realized that most of the limited amount of literature on capital punishment that I had reviewed pertains not to societies or cultures in general, but to specific types of cultures. With this insight, I was able to delineate three theories, each of which pertains to a different level of sociopolitical complexity. The correspondence between these theories and the eight political types is shown in Chapter 9. Inherent in each theory is the notion that capital punishment is a method of coping with a perceived threat to the well-being of the community.

In order to increase the information available on the 32 cultures for which my students had already found data on capital punishment, and in hopes of adding more cases to the sample, I selected additional categories—681–689 (offenses and sanctions), 691 (judicial authority), 696 (execution of justice), and 697 (prisons and jails). These additions greatly expanded the ethnographic information base that might contain data on capital punishment. I coded directly from the ethnographic sources on the 60 cultures in the PSF (summer 1981); new information was added to the code sheets of the cultures already identified as practicing capital punishment, and additional cultures were found to have capital crimes. Each crime found in a culture was examined to determine whether the offense sometimes or always resulted in capital punishment. In the fall of 1981, ten first-year graduate students, using code sheets, each coded six cultures.[4] I compared my code sheets with theirs and made any changes that were needed, either because the students had found relevant passages I had missed or because their interpretations caused me to rethink my codes. (The justification for not doing a traditional reliability check is discussed below; see Methodological Interlude.)

Data on capital punishment were found for 53 of the cultures in the PSF. Using the definition of capital punishment that is offered in Chapter 2, it was found that 51 of these cultures had capital punishment. The result, to me, was unpredicted and surprising. As already stated above, when the research was initiated, I believed that capital punishment was a phenomenon primarily restricted to states. But with 96 percent of the cultures in the sample for which there were data using the death penalty, I was forced to conclude that capital punishment is empirically a near-universal and that it might even theoretically be a cross-cultural universal. I later concluded that for the two cultures without capital punishment the data were not sufficient for determining that capital punishment was not present (see Chapter 5, pp. 40–42). Of the 7 cultures for which information was insufficient, 4 may not have capital punishment (Mataco, Pawnee, Taiwan Hokkien, and Copper Eskimo) and 3 may have capital punishment (Aymara, Central Thai, and Highland Scots). (Information found elsewhere than in the HRAF Files permits coding the Highland Scots as having capital punishment, however, [Tacitus 1872: 302].)

The coded information on the 53 cultures was recorded on a data sheet and was entered directly into a computer data file (see Appendix B). The Cyber 703 computer at the State University of New York at Buffalo was used for all analyses. All cross-tabulations (see Chapter 9) were done with the SPSS program.

METHODOLOGICAL INTERLUDE

In general, reliability means arriving at a positive answer to the following question: Will two observers obtain the same results? (This question presumes that the two observers are viewing the same object.) However, in cross-cultural research, if coders are instructed to use the HRAF Files directly, they may not read the same passages. Hence, lack of reliability in cross-cultural research may result not only from coders coding the same passages and getting different results (what is usually meant by lack of reliability) but also from coders coding from different passages.

The capital punishment study led me to discover a paradox concerning coding in cross-cultural research. Reliability is high when data are scant, and reliability is low when data are profuse. The paradox can be explained as follows: (1) If the source materials are scant on a culture, the coders are likely to find the one or two paragraphs of text that contain the data. Thus they code from the same textual material and are likely to obtain the same codes. If the data are voluminous, each coder will probably miss some relevant paragraphs. Therefore, coding a culture with many paragraphs of text on a topic introduces some unreliability, because each coder is "short" some paragraphs. Furthermore, coders, in part, may be coding from different paragraphs. (This problem can be corrected by having the coders share the available textual material.) (2) When the source materials are voluminous, it is likely that coders will miss information that is relevant to some codes because of "sensory overload." Moreover, a rich data base may provide conflicting information, sometimes even from the same publication, which is likely to lead to coding discrepancies between coders. Thus, the paradox exists that reliability is high when data are scant, and reliability is low when data are profuse. This problem can be corrected, in part, by comparing codes and reconciling discrepancies. This procedure was followed in this study.

PART II

Capital Punishment— A Universal Culture Trait

CHAPTER 4

Capital Punishment as a Legal Process

Capital punishment, the enactment of the death penalty, is the final phase of a legal process that begins with the commission of a crime. Although capital punishment is found in all societies, variations occur in the steps that compose the legal process associated with the death penalty. These variations are related to other aspects of the culture. Capital punishment, thus, is a universal that may take different forms in different types of societies.

Any criminal act occurring within a political community may be considered by the political leader or the leader of a subunit within the political community to be an offense that warrants capital punishment. If this is the case, a judicial process may be set in motion that will lead to the execution of the perpetrator of the act. But not all crimes are capital offenses, and not all capital offenses necessarily lead to the execution of the culprit. Indeed, whether the person is executed may depend upon circumstances surrounding the crime and upon the age, sex, or status of the person.

The legal process dealing with capital punishment begins with a crime and ends with an execution. This process typically consists of a series of steps. A crime is committed. If the wrongdoer is apprehended, he is likely to be held until his fate is decided. Torture may be used to extract a confession. A decision to execute or not will be made by the political leaders, a council, religious leaders, the community, or perhaps even the offender's own kin group. Reasons may be given for executing the criminal: the rationale for the execution may be simply to dispose of the wrongdoer, to punish the culprit, or to set an example to deter other members of the community. A particular location is selected for the execution, and the executioner is chosen or comes forth. A variety of ways of carrying out the death penalty can be used; the criminal may or may not be tortured before being killed. And, finally, there will be a community reaction to the execution.

Although a typical legal process leading to the enactment of the death penalty can be delineated, each political community deals with capital crimes in its own manner. Furthermore, within a particular political community, different capital crimes may evoke entirely different legal processes. A classic example is from the Trobriand Islands. These islands in Melanesia are famous in the literature of anthropology because they were studied intensively by Bronislaw Malinowski, who was one of the leading fieldworkers and social science theorists of the first half of the twentieth century. For the Trobrianders, Malinowski described two different legal processes: First, if a man insults the chief and the chief wishes his disposal, he will instruct "henchmen" to carry out the execution secretly. The killing will be done with spears, from ambush (1922: 64–65; 1921: 10; 1929: 447). Second, a person who has committed a homicide or incest is considered by all to have committed a heinous crime. If the offense becomes publicly known through accusations, the culprit will be insulted and ostracized. Shame plus cultural expectations may cause the person to take his own life by jumping in broad daylight from a tall coconut palm tree (1926: 77–80, 116–117).[1] Malinowski's nearly eye-witness account of a self-inflicted death is as follows (1926: 77–78):

> One day an outbreak of wailing and a great commotion told me that a death had occurred somewhere in the neighbourhood. I was informed that Kima'i, a young lad of my acquaintance, of sixteen or so, had fallen from a coco-nut palm and killed himself.
>
> I hastened to the next village where this had occurred, only to find the whole mortuary proceedings in progress. This was my first case of death, mourning, and burial, so that in my concern with the ethnographical aspects of the ceremonial, I forgot the circumstances of the tragedy even though one or two singular facts

occurred at the same time in the village which should have aroused my suspicions. I found that another youth had been severely wounded by some mysterious coincidence. And at the funeral there was obviously a general feeling of hostility between the village where the boy died and that into which his body was carried for burial.

Only much later was I able to discover the real meaning of these events: the boy had committed suicide. The truth was that he had broken the rules of exogamy, the partner in his crime being his maternal cousin, the daughter of his mother's sister. This had been known and generally disapproved of, but nothing was done until the girl's discarded lover, who had wanted to marry her and who felt personally injured, took the initiative. This rival threatened first to use black magic against the guilty youth, but this had not much effect. Then one evening he insulted the culprit in public— accusing him in the hearing of the whole community of incest and hurling at him certain expressions intolerable to a native.

For this there was only one remedy; only one means of escape remained to the unfortunate youth. Next morning he put on festive attire and ornamentation, climbed a coco-nut palm and addressed the community, speaking from among the palm leaves and bidding them farewell. He explained the reasons for his desperate deed and also launched forth a veiled accusation against the man who had driven him to his death, upon which it became the duty of his clansmen to avenge him. Then he wailed aloud, as is the custom, jumped from a palm some sixty feet high and was killed on the spot. There followed a fight within the village in which the rival was wounded; and the quarrel was repeated during the funeral.

In the present study, which includes the Trobrianders, 36 cultures were found to have two or more distinct tracks leading to execution. That is, there were two or more crimes that could lead to capital punishment (see Table 1). Only 15 cultures had a single crime or track leading to execution.

Ten variables were developed in the initial stage of research to reflect the various steps in the legal process leading to capital punishment. Since there have been no previous cross-cultural studies that have focused directly upon capital punishment, each of the ten variables was developed either from descriptions of executions, such as Malinowski's above, or from literature that had a bearing on the topic. The ten variables, as described on the code sheet, are given in Appendix A; the coded data may be found in Appendix B. The following discussions of each of the ten variables

TABLE 1

NUMBER OF CAPITAL CRIMES PER CULTURE

NUMBER OF CAPITAL CRIMES	NUMBER OF CULTURES
0	2
1	15
2	4
3	17
4	6
5	4
6	1
7	2
8	2
Total	53

describe the development of each variable and provide necessary definitions for each category. The frequency distribution of the coded data for each variable is also presented and discussed. Because of the exploratory nature of the research, it was necessary to have an "other" category or point on five of the variables during the coding; after coding, it was possible to eliminate two of the "other" categories.

Variable 1

"For what crimes is capital punishment used?" The initial list included seven categories of crime: (1) *Treason* refers either to the betrayal of the political community to enemies in other political communities or to insults directed to the political leader and members of his family. While current, popular use of the term treason refers to betrayal—e.g., the role that Benedict Arnold played in the American Revolution—the historical meaning pertains to acts directed toward the ruler. Edward III (1327–1377) of England defined treason by statute as "compassing or imagining the king's death, or that of his wife or eldest son, violating the wife of the king or of the heir apparent . . ." (*Oxford English Dictionary* 1971: 2291). The Trobriand example, above, is one of numerous cases that can be found in the ethnographic literature of capital punishment for insulting the ruler. (2) *Political assassination* is the killing of a political leader or of a person appointed by him. In addition to being a form of homicide, it could also be, but was not, classified as treason. (3) *Homicide* is the killing of another person, either intentionally or unintentionally. In some cultures, killing is a crime even if the death is accidental; in others, the circumstances associated with the homicide may be important in determining the punishment. Physical assault was included in this category. (4) *Stealing, burglary,* and *robbery* constitute a category that includes any wrongful taking of property. (5) *Sacrilegious acts* refer either to witchcraft (or sorcery) or to divulging religious secrets. Many peoples believe that witches or sorcerers practice malevolent acts, which bring misfortune or death to others. The execution of such evil persons occurs quite commonly. Less commonly found is the divulging, often by accident, of religious secrets. The typical situation is one in which an exclusive male organization has established a secret location at which tribal rites are carried out. If a woman discovers that location, she may be killed immediately. (6) *Sexual offenses* include adultery, incest, rape, and any other forbidden sexual act. The importance of including sexual transgressions on a roster of capital offenses has been demonstrated by Yehudi Cohen's (1969) study of state organization and the punishment of adultery, incest, and the violation of celibacy. Sociobiology's theory of parental investment also provides a rationale for examining sexual offenses, particularly adultery, in a study of capital punishment (Wilson 1975: 324–327). (7) *Desertion in war*, although closely related to treason, was included as a separate category.

Not surprisingly, homicide ranks first among these crimes in frequency, with 32 of the 51 cultures in the sample considering it a capital crime. Stealing, sacrilegious acts, and sexual offenses rank second, with 26 cultures each. Treason is considered a capital offense in 14 cultures. Only 2 cultures consider desertion in war a capital crime. And, surprisingly, only 2 cultures have the death penalty for political assassination. That figure is undoubtedly far too low. Any political community that executes for treason would probably execute for political assassination unless the assassin or his employer were to become the new political leader.[2] Eighteen cultures have one or more "other" reasons for capital punishment. These crimes are listed by culture in Table 2; this complete listing of the crimes emphasizes the wide range of acts which, in addition to the seven original categories, are considered capital offenses. Although conceptually some of the crimes could have been included with one of the seven major crimes, no effort was made to do so or to group them together into such new categories as arson, insurrection, or insanity. For the Aranda of central Australia, discovering a sacred location is listed as an "other" crime, even though it could be considered as a sacrilegious act. Sorcery, another

TABLE 2

"OTHER" CRIMES FOR WHICH CAPITAL PUNISHMENT IS USED

CULTURE	"OTHER" CRIMES
1. Amhara	Slave trading Armed banditry
2. Aranda	Discovering a sacred location
3. Ashanti	Suicide
4. Bahia Brazilians	Breach of peace, which was promised
5. Cuna	Man observing childbirth Aid to strangers Insanity Carelessness, causing houses to burn Lying to chief
6. Ganda	Police permitting prisoner to escape
7. Garo	"Many criminal acts"
8. Ifugao	Refusal to pay a debt or fine
9. Kapauku	Wife breaking a food taboo—husband dies Being responsible for starting a war Warrior breaking a taboo—father or brother dies
10. Korea	Arson
11. Kurd	Smuggling arms and ammunition
12. Masai	Arson
13. Pygmies	Failure to participate in a ceremony
14. Santal	Kidnapping
15. Shluh	Abuse of political power
16. Tikopia	Being a stranger
17. Toradja	Gross disobedience, by slaves Dangerous insanity
18. Truk	Taking a woman away from an island of prisoner women

sacrilegious act, was also a capital offense and was coded as the prevailing sacrilegious act. The Aranda view each of these offenses as separate crimes.

The manner in which data were collected on capital crimes— each offense in the political community being inspected to see if it were considered a capital offense— permits totaling the number of capital crimes for each culture. The range of capital crimes extends from 0 (for the 2 cultures that may not have capital punishment) to 8 (see Table 1). The bimodal distribution— with 15 cultures having only one capital crime and 32 cultures having three or more capital crimes— can perhaps be explained as follows: If the members of a political community view one particular crime as especially heinous, capital punishment will be used to punish and eliminate the culprit; if, on the other hand, the death penalty is seen as an available legal sanction that can be used to punish criminals, then the political community may choose several crimes as capital offenses. (As will be shown in Chapter 8, despotic states may execute for as many as 8 different crimes. All other types of political communities are divided, with some having only one capital offense, others several.)

Variable 2
"Are there facilities for holding prisoners?" There are three possible answers to this question: (1) Facilities for incarceration may not exist; or (2) if facilities exist, they may be devices like stocks or buildings, which have other purposes but which can temporarily hold the prisoner, perhaps for a few days, until his fate has been decided; or (3) permanent facilities, which include jails, small islands, isolated villages used exclusively for prisoners, and prison camps, may be used to hold criminals for an indefinite period. For the 28 cultures for which there were data, 11 cultures do not have facilities for holding prisoners, 5 cultures have temporary incarceration, and 12 cultures have permanent incarceration.

Variable 3
"Is 'judicial torture' used to obtain confessions?" Torture to obtain a confession that could be used to justify an execution is distinguished from torture that accompanies the execution itself and is intended to make death a painful experience. This distinction between "judicial torture" and *supplice*, the deliberate incorporation of elements of painful torture into capital punishment, has been made by Michel Foucault (1977: 39–47, 33–37) in his study of the evolution of the French penal system. Judicial torture may be either (1) absent or (2) present. Of the 27 cultures on which data were available, 19 cultures do not torture, and 8 cultures use judicial torture to obtain confessions.

Variable 4
"Who decides that the wrongdoer is to be executed?" (1) The political leader or a political leader of any subunit of the political

community may make the decision. (2) A deliberating body of important adults, known as a council, may render the decision. Outside the domain of the political, the right to make the decision may fall either (3) to the wrongdoer's kin group, (4) to religious practitioners, including shamans and diviners, (5) to the kin of the victim, or (6) to the community or to the section of the community that has been victimized. There may be more than one decision maker, since some political communities have two or more different legal processes and since the decision-making body can vary even for the same crime. In the distribution of frequencies, political leader ranks first, with 21 cultures having leaders who make the decision to execute. Councils make decisions to execute in 12 cultures, the wrongdoer's own kin group in 10 cultures, followed by community (victims) in 9 cultures, religious practitioners in 5 cultures, and kin of the victim in 5 cultures.

Variable 5

"What is the social context in which the execution takes place?" A typology was developed, using two dimensions: whether the execution is announced or not and whether the execution could be attended by any member of the community or only by select individuals.

	Announced	Not Announced
Open (to all)	Public	✕
Closed (with exceptions)	Private	Secret

The typology generates three categories: (1) public—anyone can attend; (2) private—special categories of persons may attend, such as officials and kin of the wrongdoer, and the execution is announced (this could be before or after the execution); and (3) secret—the execution is carried out in secret, without the kin of the wrongdoer present, and the execution is not announced.[3] (The crossed out cell on the table represents an unfeasible combination.) Public executions occur alone in 13 cultures, and secret executions occur alone in 8 cultures. However, in 4 more cultures both public and secret executions occur together, with the two types of settings resulting from the presence of two different legal processes in the political community. Private executions are found in 4 cultures.

Variable 6

"Who is the executioner?" The party who decides that the wrongdoer is to be killed is not necessarily the executioner. The list of possible executioners, however, contains four of the same categories found on the "who decides" list (Variable 4, above), plus a category for judicial suicide: (1) The political leader or an agent of the leader, who could be self-appointed, performs the execution. If the executioner is not the political leader or his agent, the privilege or onerous duty may fall either (2) to the kin of the victim or (3) to the kin of the offender. (4) Self-inflicted death, or judicial suicide, may be required of the offender. (5) And, lastly, the community or the members of the community who have been victims may themselves carry out the death sentence. More than one type of executioner may be found in a political community. There were data for 37 cultures: in 19 cultures, the political leader or his agent is the executioner; in 15 cultures, it is the victim's kin; in 13 cultures, the offender's kin; in 10 cultures, the community (victims); and in 5 cultures, death is self-inflicted.

Variable 7

"Does capital punishment deliberately incorporate elements of painful torture?" Although most of the ways of carrying out the death penalty cause pain to the condemned person, it is possible to combine deliberate torture with the execution and turn the act of capital punishment into an excruciatingly painful experience for the criminal. Thus, this variable deals not with whether capital punishment is painful, but with whether deliberate torture accompanies the execution. Foucault (1977: 33–37) called this kind of torture *supplice*. Capital punishment, then, can be (1) simply a withdrawal of the right to live or (2) *supplice*. For the 32 cultures for which there were data, 21 cultures inflict the death penalty without using torture, while 11 cultures deliberately make the execution painful.

Variable 8

"What is the manner in which the death penalty is carried out?" The initial list included seven different forms of execution: (1) decapitating (2) drowning (3) hanging or strangulating (4) burning (5) poisoning (6) incapacitating (and exposure), and (7) using weapons — such as arrows, guns, spears, or swords. Different methods may be used as punishment for the same crime, and it was expected that different methods would occasionally be used for different crimes within the same political community. By far the most frequent means of executing is with weapons—25 cultures. Hanging is used in 17 cultures. The effectiveness of weapons and hanging in causing death may account for their high frequency. Burning is used in 8 cultures, incapacitating in 8 cultures, drowning in 7 cultures, and decapitating in 3 cultures. Eight cultures have "other" means of carrying out the death penalty. These means are listed by culture in Table 3. Based on this information, new categories could be added to the variable, such as stoning and casting from a height, but the number of cases would be only two each, thus not warranting these additions. As was done with capital crimes, the number of ways in which the death penalty is carried out in each culture has been totaled. The range is from 1 to 8 (see Table 4). Of the 40 cultures for which there were data, half use only 1 means of executing. At the other end of the range, with 8 methods, there is just one culture standing alone—the Ganda of East Africa, one of the most despotic states ever to have been described in the anthropological literature (Roscoe 1911; Speke 1864).

Variable 9

"What reasons are given for capital punishment by those responsible for the execution?" The three reasons that make up the list were developed from the literature on criminal law. Textbooks and treatises on criminal law discuss the justifications for the punishment of criminals (Kadish and Paulsen 1975: 1–71; Packer 1968: 35–61). The reasons and justifications apply to all forms of

TABLE 3

"OTHER" MEANS BY WHICH THE DEATH PENALTY IS CARRIED OUT

CULTURE	"OTHER" MEANS OF EXECUTION
1. Azande	Casting from precipice
2. Cuna	Briar thrust up penis (for rape)
3. Ganda	Slow dismembering
4. Kanuri	Stoning
5. Pygmies	Beating, without use of weapons
6. Serbs	Stoning
7. Tikopia	Setting adrift
8. Trobriands	Jumping from coconut palm tree

TABLE 4

NUMBER OF WAYS IN WHICH THE DEATH PENALTY IS CARRIED OUT, PER CULTURE

NUMBER OF WAYS	NUMBER OF CULTURES
No data	11
1	20
2	10
3	5
4	2
5	1
6	1
7	0
8	1
Total	51

punishment, including the death penalty. Although these justifications pertain only to Anglo-American law, it seemed likely that all of them, along with other reasons, would be found present in many of the cultures in the sample. (1) Disposal of the wrongdoer by execution is, of course, a permanent solution to the problem of what to do about a person who commits a crime that is horrible in the eyes of the community. The intent of the community is simply to remove the wrongdoer from the community, so that he cannot repeat his offense or continue to threaten the community. (2) Revenge, as a group motive, is the desire to punish the wrongdoer because he deserves it. (3) To set an example for others, in order to dissuade them from committing the same or similar crimes, is known as general deterrence.

The discussion of deterrence, the "inhibiting effect that punishment, either actual or threatened, will have on the actions of those who are otherwise disposed to commit crimes" (Packer 1968: 39), dominates the literature on capital punishment. Most of the publications present evidence that purports to show that capital punishment either deters or does not deter criminal acts before they are committed. These studies deal with what is technically known as general deterrence, "inhibition [of the criminal] in advance by threat or example." Another form of deterrance, which is seldom discussed, is special deterrence, the "after-the-fact inhibition of the person being punished" (Packer 1968: 39). As the ultimate coercive sanction, capital punishment permanently removes the wrongdoer from the community; never again can he threaten or harm societal members or their culture. Furthermore, by executing the threatening individual, the community eliminates its fear of him. Thus, the death penalty is clearly a special deterrent. One anthropologist, Edmund Leach, asserts that an explicit theory of general deterrence is inherent in *all* legal systems; in Leach's view, legal systems are based at least in part on the assumption—accurate or otherwise—that potential wrongdoers are inhibited from breaking rules by the fear of consequences that would follow, and that the "actions of judges and policemen are based on this premise" (Leach 1977: 31).[4] Information on the effectiveness of capital punishment as a general deterrent was not available in the ethnographic literature; that is, data on crime rates and the frequency of use of the death penalty are rarely to be found in ethnographies.

Data were available for only 26 cultures; 9 of these cultures had two reasons. Disposal of the wrongdoer was the only reason for capital punishment found in 11 cultures, revenge alone was found in 4 cultures, deterrence alone in 1 culture, and 1 "other" reason alone. Combinations of two reasons included: 5 cultures with disposal and revenge, 2 cultures with disposal and deterrence, and 2 cultures with deterrence and an "other" reason (the other reason being in those cases to show the power of the king). The third "other" reason was to wipe out an insult honor.[5] If all reasons are treated as a group, the 35 reasons are distributed as follows: 18 disposal of wrongdoer, 9 revenge, 5 deterrence, 2 to show the power of the king, and 1 to wipe out an insult to honor. Since only 5 out of 26 cultures give deterrence as a reason, little support is found for Leach's statement. On the other hand, since 18 out of 26 cultures give disposal of wrongdoer as a reason, this reason approaches the status of a universal. At the time this variable was developed, it was thought that perhaps a three-step Guttmann scale would be present in the data. The steps would have been as follows: (1) disposal of wrongdoer only (2) disposal and revenge, and (3) disposal, revenge, and deterrence. If it had been present, the scale might have been correlated with level of political complexity. However, such a scale is not present.

Variable 10

"To what extent do the members of the political community accept capital punishment as an appropriate practice?" The relationship between social and legal morality has long been recognized; recently Richard Schwartz (1979, 1980) has argued that the wishes of the community do and should play a salient role in determining judicial outcomes. In particular, Schwartz focuses upon capital punishment in the United States as an example of the relationship. Thus the attitude of the community toward the death penalty can have a major influence upon the nature and frequency of capital punishment. A four-point variable was developed to measure this attitude: (1) most members of the community demand capital punishment (9 cultures); (2) capital punishment is accepted—deemed appropriate (16 cultures); (3) it is deemed inappropriate by a majority (1 culture); and (4) it is strongly resented by most (2 cultures). One additional culture, the Ifugao of the northern Philippines, combine (1) and (3), because two different legal processes are present, one for homicide and one for witchcraft. The finding that 26 out of 29 cultures have populations that favor the death penalty (combining 1 and 2) is consistent with the finding that capital punishment is universal. It would appear that legal morality as it pertains to capital punishment has a strong basis in social morality.

CHAPTER 5

The Universality of Capital Punishment

THE ORIGIN OF CAPITAL PUNISHMENT

This study concludes that capital punishment is what anthropologists have called a "cross-cultural universal" or a "universal culture trait." As such, it joins a list of other universals, such as religion and the family. George P. Murdock's classic discussion of "The Common Denominator of Cultures" (1945) or the "universal culture pattern" (Wissler 1923) enumerates approximately seventy-five culture traits that Murdock felt to be elements common to all known cultures. This list, which he regarded as incomplete, includes very general traits, such as law, as well as very specific traits, such as hair styles.

The universality of these traits has led social scientists to explain them with theories of basic impulses or drives. Franz Boas, the father of academic anthropology in the United States, has stated (1947, 2: 109): "Universally distributed forms, if not carried by early man all over the world, may be interpreted as determined by human nature." The best known of these explanatory theories is Malinowski's "scientific theory of culture" (1939, 1944). A recent statement of the approach is to be found in the writings of Ward

Goodenough (1980), a student of both Malinowski and Murdock. Murdock (1965: 51) has observed that:

> Universality is always significant to the anthropologist. Variation and differentiation in culture the world over is the rule, and whenever the anthropologist finds a custom, an activity, or an institution present in all societies from the simplest to the most complex he can only conclude that it is universal because it is genuinely useful or adaptive, so that all peoples have come by trial and error to adopt it. This is the case, for example, with such customs as the prohibition of theft, incest, and murder and with such institutions as marriage, the family, and religion.

Capital punishment is frequently the penalty that accompanies the violation of these prohibitions and of norms related to these institutions.

Capital punishment is almost undoubtedly an early culture trait. The universality of capital punishment is strong evidence that capital punishment evolved early in man's existence. As was well stated by Franz Boas, "the universal distribution of cultural achievements suggests the possibility of great antiquity" (1965: 155). Focusing on beliefs as inventions, Ruth Benedict, a student of Boas, suggested that the methodology of examining universal traits or beliefs is the only means of determining those traits or beliefs that are most ancient. Traits or beliefs that are universal or nearly universal, according to Benedict, "may have been very early inventions of the human race, 'cradle' traits which have become fundamental in all human thinking. . . . They are old, and they are universal" (1946b: 17).

Thousands of years ago, when man was at the band level of sociopolitical complexity, fear of fellow community members may have given rise to capital punishment; capital punishment was retained by peoples as they developed more complex social and political systems. As social and political systems changed, capital punishment was modified, as were other culture traits, to fit into the more complex systems that evolved.

It is reasonable to believe that capital punishment could have arisen at different places and at different times, rather than simply once; that is, capital punishment may have been independently invented a number of times as a method of coping with threats to the society. It then spread, as bands segmented and migrated to new areas. If capital punishment developed independently in several different regions, it is possible that the crimes for which capital punishment is used will cluster regionally; that is, one capital crime will be the norm for one region, while another capital crime will be the norm for another region.

THE EXECUTION OF THREATENING INDIVIDUALS

Many aspects of human behavior are responses to threats to one's individual well-being or to the well-being of one's community. Any threat—from supernatural beings, animals, natural events, or human beings—may lead individuals and political communities to devise means for coping with the perceived threat. Examples abound: Nations build armies to protect themselves from possible attacks by neighbors; people undergo innoculations to avoid typhoid fever; the devout offer prayers to ensure that the fires of hell will not punish them for eternity.

Capital punishment is a response to a threat. If an individual commits an act that threatens the lives of community members or the structure and continued existence of the community itself, his behavior may evoke sanctions. The threatening individual may be removed from the community, whether it be a hunting and gathering band or a large political community. The usual means by which he is removed is execution. (Alternatives are discussed below.) It seems to follow that capital punishment should be either a near-universal or a universal, provided that wrongdoers—threatening individuals—occur in all societies.[1]

Individuals who threaten others through their criminal acts are probably found in all cultures. Moreover a culture can create wrongdoers by attributing threatening acts to individuals who have committed no crimes. It is possible to have a culture in which no one has committed a crime, and yet criminals exist, because societal members from time to time have labeled some individuals as wrongdoers. The labeling of some individuals as criminals would provide individuals who pose perceived threats. A belief in witches and witchcraft is a prime example of such perceptions. No suggestion is being made here that a culture must have executions, and therefore that some societal members must be labeled as criminals (e.g., witches) in order to create "victims" for the executioner. It is simply being pointed out that individuals who have not committed crimes may be considered criminals—criminals who evoke fear and who are subject to execution.

Capital punishment has been defined as the appropriate killing within a political community of a person who has committed a crime (see Chapter 2). It is a means of eliminating an individual who poses a threat to the well-being of a political community or a local group within a political community. If some of the members of the community see a person as a threat because of what he has done, they may set in motion a legal process that ends in the execution of the threatening individual. In other words, capital punishment is a final solution to a community problem.[2] The availability of tools and implements that can be used as weapons makes executions feasible in all cultures. Functional alternatives appear to exist for dealing with the dangerous individual: (1) Those who fear the individual may exit. The culprit is left alone. If he has relatives and friends, they may stay with him. (2) Physical incapacitation, ranging from crippling to imprisonment, may be inflicted. (3) Exiling may take place. In some cultures, exile is equivalent to the death penalty, because a person alone either cannot survive or will be killed by strangers. However, these alternatives are not final—the dangerous individual may return, perhaps with supporters, or engage in additional behavior that is harmful to the community, such as sorcery. Thus, the need to eliminate the source of the threat and the finality of killing the threatening person may give rise to capital punishment. A series of findings, based on this cross-cultural study, provide support for the above generalizations.

Capital punishment is a cross-cultural universal. Of the 53 countries for which there initially appeared to be data on capital punishment, 51 cultures employ the death penalty for at least one crime. (For a brief discussion of the 7 cultures for which there was insufficient information, see Chapter 3, Methodology.) In only 2 cultures, those of the Andamans and the Bororo, does it appear that capital punishment may not exist. Clearly and, indeed, spectacularly, capital punishment is found to be empirically a near-universal. The data show that for each of the 51 cultures, capital punishment is a culture trait; it is a sanction in place, ready to be used, if political leaders—or political leaders together with the population—wish it to be used. In all ethnographic descriptions, capital punishment seems to have been actually used, rather than to be a practice that people reported but did not use.

Neither of the 2 cultures that appear not to have capital punishment present completely convincing data that capital punishment is absent. For both the Andamans and the Bororo, first-contact information is scant; that is, the first ethnographic reports contain little information on legal procedures. The passages from which the codings of no capital punishment were made are general statements, made by twentieth-century ethnographers, who studied these cultures after they had been subjugated by modern states. These ethnographers appear to be relying for their judgments upon other people's first-contact information. For the Andamanese, a band-level society who occupy several islands in the Bay of Bengal, A. R. Radcliffe-Brown (1964: 48) states: "There does not appear to have been in the Andamans any such thing as the punishment of crime." Although Radcliffe-Brown is considered a leading figure in anthropology, because of his theoretical contributions to functional theory, he was by his own admission a less than fully competent fieldworker. In his study of the Andamans, he states that he did not have time to become "expert" in the language, and that during the fieldwork period he was "inexperienced in the use of the genealogical method" (1964: 69, 72) — a remarkable admission, considering that his mentor, W. H. R. Rivers, himself developed the genealogical method (Slobodin 1978: 40, 48–49). Throughout his ethnography, Radcliffe-Brown relies heavily upon E. H. Man (1932), the major nineteenth-century source for the Andamans. Unfortunately, Man himself does not provide any information on capital punishment.

The data are similarly scant for the Bororo, a tribal people without councils, who live in the Matto Grosso region of Brazil. Feuding occurs between kinship groups: "Even murder, instead of being punished, merely evokes a feud" (Lowie 1946: 427). Further, Colbacchini and Albisetti (1942: 135) have written: "There is among them neither judge nor penalities; the only sanction is the public reprobation done by the chiefs of the aldeia. . . . Scorn as maximum social punishment is greatly feared. . . ." Data are seemingly not available on offenses within the kin group, the one area in which capital punishment is likely to occur in tribes that do not have councils but do have feuding (see Chapter 7).

If the Andamans and the Bororo were to be dropped from the sample for lack of data on capital punishment—and there certainly are grounds for doing so—there would be data on only 51 cultures, all 51 of which have capital punishment. For the sake of methodological rigor, the cultures were not dropped. It is not a sound research procedure to recode examples that do not fit the theory that emerges from one's research. My initial theory predicted that we would find that some small-scale societies do not have capital punishment (see Chapter 3). If I had not been seeking—and seeking hard—for small-scale societies without capital punishment, I would surely have dropped initially both the Andamans and the Bororo for lack of data. Thus the empirical result obtained is that capital punishment is a near-universal. If, however, the Andamans and the Bororo were dropped, then capital punishment would become a cross-cultural universal in this sample.

Except for these 2 cultures, no cultures without capital punishment in the ethnographic record have come to my attention. Some Western industrial nations are reported as not having capital punishment, a claim that may be correct for some polities. The reports usually emanate from newspapers or television; colleagues who are familiar with contemporary European cultures make similar claims. The validity of these claims can be questioned. It was noted in Chapter 2 (p. 13) that the absence of capital punishment for a brief period is not sufficient reason to classify a political community as without capital punishment; after a 10-year suspension of executions several states in the United States reinstituted capital punishment. It was also noted in Chapter 2 (pp. 12–13) that the execution of war captives is a form of capital punishment. The execution of German and Japanese officials after World War II provides examples of Western industrial nations having capital punishment. Although the federal government under civil authority in the United States executed only 33 persons between 1930 and 1963 (U.S. Department of Justice 1976: 55), the United States, in conjunction with its allies, did impose capital punishment upon both German and Japanese war criminals following World War II. Between 1946 and 1949, 10 Germans were hanged and 720 Japanese executed (Morris 1976: 462). In May 1960, Israeli agents seized Adolf Eichmann in Buenos Aires, Argentina, and transported him to Israel to stand trial. Two years later, an Israeli court found him guilty of committing numerous crimes during World War II and ordered that he be executed by hanging (Arendt 1963: 240–298).

Although a thorough literature search has not been made, the examples of Western industrial nations that have been examined provide evidence that laws prohibiting capital punishment can be set aside when it is in the interest of the nation to do so. The case of Switzerland is instructive in this regard. Prior to 1942, each canton of Switzerland had its own criminal laws; some included the death penalty. The Swiss Criminal Code, put into force in 1942, abolished the death penalty except in time of war, when, under the Swiss Military Code, the death penalty can be imposed (Clinard 1978: 46). Spain has a similar statute. Article 15 of Spain's new constitution reads: "The death penalty remains abolished, except for possible provisions in the military penal code during war time" (Sellin 1980:

179). Although these are "laws on the books," the presence of which does not prove the existence of capital punishment (see Chapter 2, p. 13), there seems to be little doubt from the way the statutes were developed that, if war occurred, the death penalty would be used for military crimes such as desertion or treason. Without adequate information on any culture without capital punishment, it can be concluded with some degree of confidence that capital punishment is a universal culture trait.

Crimes that directly threaten individuals and their community—homicide, stealing, and violations of community religious norms—are those most likely to lead to capital punishment. Homicide ranks first among capital crimes, with 32 cultures out of 51 cultures (61 percent) considering that homicide should lead to the death penalty (see Chapter 4, Variable 1, p. 26). Stealing, sacrilegious acts, and sexual offenses rank second, with 26 cultures each (51 percent). In 14 cultures, treason is a capital offense (27 percent). Many other crimes for which the death penalty is used are found in the ethnographic literature (see Table 2, Chapter 4). However, by far the most prevalent capital crimes— homicide, stealing, religious violations, and sexual offenses— are those acts which most directly threaten people.

Some regional differences in capital crimes occur. Table 5, made up of five smaller tables, shows the regional patterning. Homicide is most likely to be found as a capital offense in Africa, the Mediterranean, and Eurasia; stealing, in Africa and the Mediterranean; sacrilegious acts, in North America, Africa, and Oceania; sexual offenses, in the Mediterranean, Eurasia, and Oceania; and treason, in Oceania. If capital punishment is an early culture trait, which seems highly likely, it was probably independently invented in several world regions to dispose of wrongdoers who engaged in those acts which most threatened the community or frightened the people. In other words, infractions against those norms of society which were deemed most important by the people were punished most severely, usually by capital punishment. Since the norms that are deemed most important may vary from culture to culture, it is to be expected that what is considered a capital crime will vary from culture to culture. The segmentation and migration of cultures throughout a major geographic region would account for the higher frequency of a particular capital offense in that geographic region.

The major reason for capital punishment given by the members of a culture is "disposal of the wrongdoer." The reason for such an

TABLE 5

REGIONAL DIFFERENCES FOR CAPITAL CRIMES

Homicide

	Africa, Mediterranean, Eurasia	North America, South America, Oceania
Yes	21	11
No	5	14

Stealing

	Africa, Mediterranean	All others
Yes	12	14
No	5	20

Sacrilegious Acts

	North America, Africa, Oceania	South America, Mediterranean, Eurasia
Yes	18	8
No	8	17

Sexual Offenses

	Mediterranean, Eurasia, Oceania	North America, South America, Africa
Yes	17	9
No	9	16

Treason

	Oceania	All others
Yes	5	9
No	4	33

execution is to remove a menace from their midst. It is not for revenge or to set an example for others. Of the several reasons given for capital punishment, by far the most common reason is disposal of the wrongdoer: of the 26 cultures for which there are data, 18 (60 percent) have this as a reason (see Chapter 4, variable 9, p. 32) The next most frequently mentioned reason is revenge, with 9 cases.

Capital punishment is accepted as an appropriate practice by most members of the community or political community. Of 29 cultures with data on community reactions to capital punishment, 26 have populations which either demand (10 cultures) or accept (16 cultures) the death penalty (see Chapter 4, Variable 10, p. 34). Thus, 90 percent of the cultures in the sample for which there are data have members who favor capital punishment.

In conclusion, the findings of the cross-cultural study support the view that capital punishment is a response to an individual who has threatened the lives of community members and the continued existence of the community itself. Capital punishment removes the threatening individual from the community. The findings support this view: (1) Capital punishment is a cross-cultural universal. Although exceptions may exist, the evidence shows that most, if not all, societies, at one time or another, will use the death penalty. (2) Capital crimes are most likely to be offenses that directly threaten people—homicide, stealing, religious violations, and sexual offenses. (3) Disposal of the wrongdoer is the reason most frequently found for executing a community member. (4) Most members of a community or political community accept capital punishment as an appropriate sanction.

PART III

Capital Punishment and Political Systems: Theories

Three specific theories are developed in Part 3: group survival theory (Chapter 6), confrontation theory (Chapter 7), and political legitimacy theory (Chapter 8). Each of these specific theories addresses itself to the question of why political leaders and communities use the death penalty. Common to all three theories is the element of threat: a dangerous individual threatens the political leader and other members of a political community by his actions; that threat galvanizes the political leader or the members of the community to engage in the task of executing a fellow community member or a stranger. The three theories are quite different: one deals with incest and other group-threatening acts; another with the connivance of political leaders in killings; and the third with political terror. The apparent differences arise largely from the societal unit to which they apply; the three theories pertain to three different levels of sociopolitical complexity—bands, tribes, and states. In spite of the differences in the theories, each theory contains within it, in some form, the notion that a dangerous individual must be disposed of through the use of the death penalty. Each of the three specific theories is itself the result of combining several studies that contain similar theoretical ideas. This synthesizing task was not difficult, because the studies in most instances pertain to one specific type of culture.

A typology of political systems was developed explicitly for this study; the types were delineated as the coding of ethnographic data was in progress. The typology is a refinement and an elaboration of a classification scheme that has been in use for over twenty years. Elman Service's (1962) four types of sociopolitical systems—bands, tribes, chiefdoms, and states—provided a starting point. It then became necessary to elaborate, in order to test the theories that were being developed: the tribe and state categories were each subdivided into three types. And in order to test confrontation theory, it was necessary to distinguish between tribes with feuding and those without feuding, as well as to consider whether councils were present. The no council, no feuding category was integrated into the definition of the band type; this type was used to test group survival theory. Again, in order to test political legitimacy theory, it was necessary to divide states into two categories—despotic states and mature states; a third category then emerged—dependent native peoples. Chiefdoms were grouped with states as a fourth category.

CHAPTER 6

Group Survival Theory: Capital Punishment in Bands

Any act that is seen by the members of a band as threatening the survival of their group will subject the perpetrator of that act to capital punishment. This theory seems to have originated in Émile Durkheim's theory of penal evolution (1973). In the simpler societies, according to Durkheim, offenses against the "conscience collective"—public authority, mores, religion, and venerated objects —evoke harsh punishment; such punishment consists of mutilation and capital punishment involving torture. This theory is referred to by Inverarity and Lauderdale as "Durkheim's concept of repressive justice" (1983: 286–289).

The band is "the simplest, most rudimentary form of social structure" (Service 1962: 107). The band itself is a group made up of related nuclear families. Although there may be many culturally similar bands, the individual band is the structure within which all political, economic, and religious activities are organized and carried out. The band itself, then, is the political, the economic, and the religious organization for its members.

As societies evolve, according to Durkheim's theory, the collective sentiments, which are strong in band-level societies, diminish; crime against persons increases, while religious forms of criminality decline. Thus the repressive or penal sanctions found in band-level societies gave way to restitutive sanctions. Spitzer (1979) refers to Durkheim's theory as "The Organic Differentiation Hypothesis" and provides a critique; several anthropologists cited by Spitzer point out that, contrary to Durkheim, restitutive sanctions rather than penal sanctions are typically found in simple societies. However, in support of Durkheim, it can be pointed out that there are simple societies in which repressive sanctions are found, and that some of these societies were known to him.

Durkheim appears to have used the central Australians as a case study from which he drew many of his ideas on crime. In his studies of religion, this indebtedness is clear (Durkheim and Mauss 1963). One Australian group, the Aranda, have been among the best-known "primitive" societies since the late nineteenth century (Spencer and Gillen 1899). They are included in the sample used in this study. These band-level peoples had a complicated kinship system, with strict marriage laws that required an individual to choose a marriage partner from a particular kinship group. To have sexual relations with a person not of the prescribed group was regarded as incest and was punished by death. The elders of the band decided in secret upon the execution and asked a neighboring band to carry out the sentence of death (Spencer and Gillen 1927: 443–453). Also punished by death were sorcery and the endangering of sacred objects (Spencer and Gillen 1927: 403, 111).

Two anthropologists, Leslie White and Edmund Leach, presumably influenced by Durkheim as well as by the ethnographic description of Aranda incest and capital punishment, have presented theories that argue that incest was so disruptive of social order in early and simple societies that it had to be prevented, either by execution of the culprits (White) or through negative supernatural sanctions (Leach). White first set forth his theory in 1948 (1949: 327). His most recent statement appears in a posthumously published volume (1975: 32):

> The prohibition of incest is the first identifiable act in human history. It is the first instance of the subordination of the desire of the individual to the common good. As such, it is the first ethical act of history. The incest taboo marks the beginning of human social evolution. Had not interfamiliar marriage unions been made mandatory, social evolution would have been impossible.

The foregoing theory receives support from facts pertaining to the punishment meted out to offenders. The incest taboo is found on the lowest known levels of cultural development. It was almost invariably punished by death. The reason was that incest was a blow struck at the very foundations of human society in the early stages of its development.

Leach's theory appeared in a lecture on primitive law (1977: 31–32):

> As between one society and another the varieties of sin will differ but it is nearly always the case that the taboos which are most strongly supported by supernatural sanctions are those connected with sex and kinship. Incest rather than murder is the ultimate prototype of a public crime. Incest taboos of one kind or another can be identified in all kinds of society but it is only in small scale communities, where kinship is all pervading, that the offence of incest acquires an absolute priority of seriousness over all other potential breaches of the rules.
>
> This should not surprise us . . . incest is the supreme threat to the fabric of society because it confuses the distinction between kinship roles.

Both sanctions—capital punishment and negative supernatural sanctions—are combined in a similar theory by Colin Turnbull. However, blasphemy, rather than incest, is the crime that turns community members against the offender (1978: 55):

> As an anthropologist I cannot avoid remarking on the absence of such a phenomenon [brutalization] in primitive society, where the death penalty is generally not given for offenses against individuals, but only for offenses that threaten the total society. We would call it treason, but in small-scale societies, "blasphemy" would be a better word, referring to any act that could invoke the wrath of the divine against the entire society. Even then, such an act, being more in the nature of a sin than a crime, cannot be corrected by punishment alone. Since the offense was against God, punishment should be left to God; thus we get the invocation of "supernatural sanctions." Atonement is imperative and possible, for the focus is positive, on the good of the total society, rather than negative, on the mere destruction of a single offender; this requires divine intervention rather than punishment. Where it exists in such societies, the death penalty is then a part of the ritual process of appealing to the divine and is totally devoid of the violent demand for retribution found in our society.

Turnbull's theory has probably been influenced by his extensive fieldwork with the Pgymies of the Congo. The Pgymies, as well as the Aranda, are a society in the sample. The Pgymies execute sorcerers (Turnbull 1965: 236), incorrigible thieves (1965: 186), and those hunters who do not participate in prehunt ceremonies (1965: 190), an act which can be classified as blasphemy:

> . . . the direct threat of death . . . is reserved among the Eulu Mbuti and other net-hunting bands uniquely for the crime of failure on the part of an adult male to sing (a crime sometimes conversely described as sleeping) during the molimo festival. . . . It is said that anyone found sleeping (the only conceivable reason for not singing) would be killed with two spears in the stomach and buried beneath the molimo hearth. The women would simply be told he had gone away, or been taken by a leopard, and he would never be referred to again.

Incest is dealt with through ostracism—"the offender will be left alone in the forest, and alone he will die" (1965: 190).

A similar theory, but one that does not focus upon incest or blasphemy as the reason for execution, has been set forth by Karl N. Llewellyn and E. Adamson Hoebel (1941: 140–146, 178, 327; Hoebel 1954: 88–92). In the classic ethnography, *The Cheyenne Way*, Llewellyn and Hoebel (1941) describe a trouble case, Case 20, in which a Cheyenne Indian who had killed twice was killed by a man who feared being killed by him. The "executioner" was encouraged and assisted by his warrior society, the Dog Soldiers, in setting up an ambush. The case, which is reported in Grinnell's *The Cheyenne Indians* (1923, 1: 230–353), describes the two killings and the execution in great detail. The entire case is presented below:

> The death of Walking Coyote in 1855 and the events connected with it show something of how quarrels, fights, and killings occasionally took place in the Cheyenne camp.
>
> In the year 1854, White Horse, then chief of the Fox Soldiers, stole the wife of Walking Coyote, who was very fond of her and brooded much over the trouble. He sent word to White Horse to send back the woman, saying that if he did not do so he would kill him. No attention was paid to the message, and after a time Walking Coyote went to Yellow Wolf, who had adopted him, and said: "Father, as you know, White Horse has stolen my woman and I have sent word to him many times to send her back, but he does not do so. Now I intend to kill him, and I ask you not to interfere with my trouble, not to ask me to refrain from killing this man."
>
> Walking Coyote knew that Yellow Wolf loved him better than he did any of his own sons and daughters, and he suspected that Yellow Wolf might ask him not to take revenge on White Horse,

and if Yellow Wolf asked this, Walking Coyote felt he must obey him.

One day in the summer of 1854 Walking Coyote with War Bonnet rode up to St. Vrain's Fort (on the South Fork of Platte River in Colorado) from their camp twenty miles below. White Horse was living in a camp of Cheyennes there. Walking Coyote rode into the fort and saw White Horse and his wife—not the woman who had been stolen—sitting on a bench in the hall of the fort. When the two saw Walking Coyote, they arose and walked toward the hands' messroom, and Walking Coyote jumped off his horse and shot White Horse with his gun, the ball passing through the upper part of the chest and killing him at once. Then Walking Coyote and War Bonnet led their horses outside the gate of the fort, and sat down there, and Walking Coyote said, "If anyone has anything to say to me, I am here."

After they had sat there for a short time, Little Wolf, a cousin of Yellow Wolf, came out and said to Walking Coyote, "This is all over with; you should now go back to your camp." The two men mounted and rode to camp.

Shortly after this the woman returned to Walking Coyote's lodge. After this killing, Winnebago (*Nahk' to wŭn*) renewed the arrows because of the killing. A little later he stole from Walking Coyote the woman that White Horse had stolen and went up north with her.

Walking Coyote sent word to him, saying, "I am not going to kill another man for this woman, but I shall take your wife, Spirit Woman" (*A si' mŏn i*). Before Nahktowun returned from the North, Walking Coyote went to Nahktowun's lodge, and, entering, took Spirit Woman by the arm and said, "Come along now!" She went with him, for she feared him.

When Nahktowun returned from the North and found what had happened, he was angry, so that night he took his gun, went to the lodge of Walking Coyote, looked in at the door, saw him sitting on his bed, where he was resting after returning from the buffalo hunt, and putting the muzzle of his gun through the door he shot Walking Coyote, killing him.

Next morning he went again to Walking Coyote's lodge, took Asimoni, and made her go back to his lodge.

After the killing of Walking Coyote the arrows were renewed, perhaps by Red Moon.

One day, eight years later, in the spring of 1863, Nahktowun was sitting behind his lodge filing arrowpoints, which he had fastened into a cottonwood stick to hold them. While he was doing this Kutenim came up and began to discuss with him the question of a horse, the ownership of which had been in dispute between the two. Kutenim was a distant relative of White Horse. As Nahktowun was working away, Kutenim became more angry at him and abused him, and finally Nahktowun jumped to his feet and raising the stick which he had been using to file his arrowpoints, struck Kutenim on the head with it and knocked him down. Kutenim jumped up and ran to his lodge, which was near by, to get his rifle, while Nahktowun strung his bow and took a handful of arrows from his quiver. Presently Kutenim ran out of his lodge and fired at Nahktowun, and the ball passed close to his head. Nahktowun drew his bow and shot Kutenim in the left breast. Kutenim dropped his gun, and drawing his butcher knife, rushed at Nahktowun, who ran away, but Kutenim overtook him and slashed him on the arm, and then fell dead.

The men around about, seeing what had happened, did not go near the two. Only old women and old men ran up to them.

The Bowstring Soldiers, who then had charge of the camp, wanted to punish Nahktowun for killing Kutenim by whipping him. They consulted the chiefs, who advised them not to notice the affair at all, and nothing was done to Nahktowun.

The arrows were renewed not long afterward.

In the summer of 1864 Nahktowun was living with the Arapahoes. He had an Arapaho woman, and some people began to talk as if Rising Fire, *Ho ist o' ha a* (Smoke Rising), were trying to steal the woman. This made Rising Fire unhappy, and the more he thought of it the worse he felt, and the angrier he became toward Nahktowun. Finally he said to some of his friends, "I shall have to kill Nahktowun; he killed my cousin and now he is talking about me."

His friends replied: "You ought to do so, because if you do not kill him, he will kill you. He has already killed two men and is an outlaw, and if he feels like it he may cut your throat or shoot you."

Not long after this, Nahktowun, who was a Dog Soldier, was invited by one of the Dog Soldiers to come over and eat at his lodge. He therefore moved over from the Arapaho camp near Fort Larned on the Arkansas and camped with the Cheyennes who were on the Saline. On the day of the feast he started, with Little Robe and Good Bear, to walk to the lodge of the host. On their way they passed the lodge of Rising Fire, who was sitting inside looking out the door, and as they passed he shot Nahktowun with a gun and broke his spine. When Nahktowun fell, Little Robe and Good Bear stepped to one side, and Little Robe called out to Rising Fire, "Well, you have begun your work; now come out and finish it."

Rising Fire took an old brass-mounted horse pistol, walked over to where Nahktowun lay, and blew out his brains. *Mĕhhĭm' ik* (Eagle's Head) renewed the arrows on the Solomon.

Llewellyn and Hoebel conclude that the Cheyenne distinguished between "murderers and bully-murderers" (1941: 144) and that the Cheyenne killer "had twice demonstrated that the religious and legal injunctions meant nothing to him. The circumstances of his death have all the marks of a social conspiracy" (1941: 146). Although the case is treated as "deviational" (1941: 178) and as demonstrating that "normal homicide machinery had failed to work regeneration upon a particular man" (1941: 327), Case 20 seems to be a socially sanctioned execution of a killer who is feared by the community. In other words, it describes a case of capital punishment.

Hoebel, in *The Law of Primitive Man* (1954), quotes the now well-known case of a Cumberland Sound Eskimo who had killed three men.[1] The case is taken from Franz Boas' classic ethnography, *The Central Eskimo* (1888: 668):

> The fact that the custom is found among tribes so widely separated will justify a description of those events which came under my own observation. There was a native of Padli by the name of Padlu. He had induced the wife of a Cumberland Sound native to desert her husband and follow him. The deserted husband, meditating revenge, cut off the upper part of the barrel of his gun so that he could conceal it under his jacket. He crossed the land and visited his friends in Padli, but before he could accomplish his intention of killing Padlu the latter shot him. When this news was reported in Qeqerten, the brother of the murdered man went to Padli to avenge the death of his brother; but he also was killed by Padlu. A third native of Cumberland Sound, who wished to avenge the death of his relatives, was also murdered by him. On account of all these outrages the natives wanted to get rid of Padlu, but yet they did not dare to attack him. When the pimain [headman] of the Akudnirmiut in Niaqonaujang learned of these events he started southward and asked every man in Padli whether Padlu should be killed. All agreed; so he went with the latter deer hunting in the upper part of Pangnirtung, northwest of Padli, and near the head of the fjord he shot Padlu in the back.

Hoebel interprets this Eskimo case and others in this manner (1954: 88–89):

> The homicidal recidivist . . . becomes a social menace liable at any time to strike down another victim. As a general menace, he becomes a public enemy. As a public enemy, he becomes the object of public action. The action is legal execution. . . . Repeated

murder becomes a public crime punishable by death at the hands of an agent of the community. . . . The important element is that the executioner, who undertakes the slaying, seeks and obtains, in advance, community approval for his act of riddance. When such approval is obtained no blood revenge may be taken on the executioner. . . . Furthermore, revenge is precluded for the simple reason that unanimous consent involves also the consent of the murderer's relatives, if any be in the community.

The !Kung Bushmen, who, like the Aranda, the Pgymies, the Cheyenne, and the Central Eskimo, are among the best known of band-level societies, provide yet another example of capital punishment in bands. In a recent study, Richard B. Lee describes four !Kung killings as executions (1984: 96). His discussion constitutes another formulation of group survival theory (1984: 95–96):

> The prevalence of feuds brings us back to our original question: Once the pandora's box of violence is opened, how is it possible for people to close it down again in the absence of the state or an overriding outside political authority?
>
> The !Kung do have one method of last resort, a trump card, for bringing a string of homicides to an end. I listened with amazement to my informant Debe as he unfolded an incredible tale of passion and revenge. . . .
>
>> After my father's murder, Debe, a man who was my !kun!a [older namesake] complained, "Now my namesake Debe has no father, but Samkau still has a father. Why is this?"
>>
>> I said, "You are right. I am going to kill Bo, who started it all."
>>
>> "No," Debe said, "Bo is just a youngster, but Gau is a senior man, a n!ore owner, and he is the one who has killed another n!ore owner, Hxome. I am gong to kill him so that n!ore owners will be dead on both sides."
>>
>> One evening Debe walked right into Gau's camp and without saying a word shot three arrows into Gau, one in the left shoulder, one in the forehead, and a third in the chest. Gau's people made no move to protect him. After the three arrows were shot, Gau still sat facing the attacker. Then Debe raised his spear as if to stab him. But Gau said, "You have hit me three times. Isn't that enough to kill me, that you want to stab me too?"
>>
>> When Gau tried to dodge away from the spear, Gau's people came forward to disarm Debe of his spear. Having been so badly wounded, Gau died quickly, but made no further move to harm Debe. However, fearing more trouble,

some of our people brought in the Tswana man Isak to mediate the dispute.

The only word to describe the events above is an execution. There is no other explanation for the fact that Gau's people made no move to aid him as Debe walked into camp and killed him. This was not an isolated case: a similar outcome ended the careers of three other men, all of whom had killed before.

In the most dramatic case on record, a man named /Twi had killed three other people, when the community, in a rare move of unanimity, ambushed and fatally wounded him in full daylight. As he lay dying, all the men fired at him with poisoned arrows until, in the words of one informant, "he looked like a porcupine." Then, after he was dead, all the women as well as the men approached his body and stabbed him with spears, symbolically sharing the responsibility for his death.

I find this image striking. It is as if for one brief moment, this egalitarian society constituted itself a state and took upon itself the powers of life and death. It is this collective will in embryo that later grew to become the form of society that we know today as the state.

Group survival theory, as formulated by Durkheim, White, Leach, Turnbull, Llewellyn, Hoebel, and Lee, pertains to societies at the band level of sociopolitical complexity. The theory posits a small, culturally homogeneous political community, in which everyone knows everyone else (i.e., a primary group). If any member threatens the survival of the band by acts that disrupt the social or religious order (Durkheim considered these the same), or that endanger the band's ability to obtain food, or deprive members of their lives, that member will be disposed of. The possibility also exists that a stranger (i.e., a person who is not a member of the community) living with the band may be executed if he threatens the survival of the group. Since the offense is a community concern, the decision to execute is made by the community as a whole, or certainly by all of the elders. An ambush with weapons, sometimes in the hands of members of another political community, completes the legal process.

This same process, however, occurs in local groups within political communities much larger and more complex than bands. Joseph Westermeyer's case study of "assassination and conflict resolution in Laos" (1973) is an excellent example. The first six of Westermeyer's ten cases are capital punishment, as defined in Chapter 2. A community member ambushes a recidivist criminal or witch. The homicides are not political assassinations, because the victims are not politically important persons, and the killings are "publicly sanctioned deaths" (1973: 130). The homicides meet the definition of capital punishment, since the killings are considered appropriate, and there are reasons for the killings (i.e., the victim is a criminal or witch). These homicides are the executions of troublemakers. Local authorities condone the killings; authorities at higher levels of government either are unaware of the homicides or else they ignore them. Westermeyer's remaining four cases are killings of important persons: one was a political leader, two were military/police, and one was an American advisor. They abused their authority, according to Westermeyer. Although there were reasons for these four homicides, and the deaths were publicly sanctioned at the local level, it is difficult to classify them as capital punishment, since the larger political unit to which the victims belonged surely did not sanction or condone the homicides. From the point of view of the local group, these killings were justifiable (i.e., capital punishment); from the point of view of the Laotian government, they were political assassinations.

Executions of this nature probably occur in small local or primary groups within centralized political systems throughout the world. Regardless of a government's attitude—from tacit approval to condemnation—the practices will occur. Kressel's (1981) study of intrafamily homicide for family honor in Arab Muslim culture is set within the modern state of Israel; the killings of female kin took place between 1973 and 1977. The killing of a recidivist "criminal" recently occurred in a small community in the United States. On July 10, 1981, Ken McElroy was shot repeatedly by one or more persons at midday in front of perhaps as many as sixty people in Skidmore, Missouri. No one admits to seeing who fired the shots, and many town members publicly stated that they would not turn the person in if they did know. McElroy was the town bully: he repeatedly threatened people with guns, he had wounded two men, and he had forced the local marshal to resign at gunpoint. Although charged with perhaps two dozen felony counts over the years, he was only once found guilty. The people of Skidmore were afraid to testify against him. Out on $40,000 bond, he violated his bond arrangement by carrying firearms. A number of citizens signed a complaint, and then the bond hearing scheduled for July 10—the day on which he was shot—was postponed. The fearful residents walked to a bar where McElroy and his wife were known to be, then followed the McElroys to their truck. While he was seated in the truck, Ken McElroy was shot to death. McElroy's wife said, "I seen a man go across the street, go into his pickup, take the gun out, and I seen him shoot it" ("60 Minutes," January 31, 1982—transcript courtesy of CBS News; Reese and Monroe 1981).

To summarize, a repeat offender, or one who with one act threatens the safety or livelihood of the local group, is likely to be executed whether the offender is a member of a band or belongs to a community within a state. In the former case, the execution is clearly capital punishment; in the latter case, if the killing is tacitly approved by the political leaders, it, too, is capital punishment However, if the killing is strongly disapproved, it is murder or political assassination, depending upon the status of the victim. At the band level, the local group and the political community are coterminous; the interests of both groups are identical. At higher levels of sociopolitical complexity, the local group and the political community are different, but the need of the local group to rid itself of individuals who threaten the community persists. At the tribal level, the kinship group will execute its own members, often after strong pressure from the political leader (see Confrontation Theory, Chapter 7). At the state level, the killing becomes nonlegal from the point of view of the political leaders, unless they approve or condone the killing. As was the case in Skidmore, Missouri, communities will dispose of threatening individuals, and local leaders will approve; thus, the execution is legal from the point of view of local leaders. At the level of state government, it is murder. But if the state of Missouri tacitly approved of the shooting of McElroy—which it did not—the killing would be classifiable as capital punishment.[2] If a situation develops within a state in which political assassination has the approval of local leaders but is strongly dissapproved by the central administration, the conditions are conducive to insurgency, uprising, and civil war. A despotic state is likely to reemerge; local leaders may be arrested and executed in order to reestablish the political supremacy of the central government (see Political Legitimacy Theory, Chapter 8).

Group survival theory, when used in conjunction with band society, leads to a set of predictions about the nature of capital punishment as it occurs in bands. If the data presented in Chapter 9 conform to the predictions, support for group survival theory is obtained. The predictions are quite specific as to the variations in the steps in the legal process pertaining to capital punishment.

> *Bands.* Those offenses which endanger the group—incest, sacrilegious acts (such as sorcery, witchcraft, and violations of taboos),

CHAPTER 7

Confrontation Theory: Capital Punishment in Tribes

FRATERNAL INTEREST GROUPS IN CONFRONTATION

From fraternal interest group theory, developed by H. U. E. Thoden van Velzen and W. van Wetering (1960) and by Keith F. Otterbein and Charlotte Swanson Otterbein (1965), can be devised a "confrontation theory": not only are fraternal interest groups pitted against each other but political leaders also find themselves in confrontation with fraternal interest groups. Fraternal interest group theory was first developed by Thoden van Velzen and van Wetering to explain why the local groups of some cultures are peaceful internally, while others are rife with internal dissension. They argued that a fraternal interest group, which is a power group of related males, resorts to aggression when there is a threat to the interests of one of its members; in societies with power groups, any act of violence will be followed by another act of violence, thereby eliciting a chain reaction. The individual who is a member of a power group acts with the assurance that his group is ready to support him and his interests, "through thick and thin." Thus, any individual act of violence can lead to conflict between fraternal interest groups, and much intrasocietal aggression can be attributed to the power groups and their struggles for power. In contrast there is no such struggle for power in societies without fraternal interest groups, and differences in power consist primarily in differences in "muscular strength and personality." Without the presence of power groups, potential combatants lack psychological support for their acts of aggression; bystanders, instead of supporting violence, may try to avert it (Thoden van Velzen and van Wetering 1960: 179–180). Thus, the difference between peaceful and nonpeaceful local groups was explained by Thoden van Velzen and van Wetering in terms of a single independent variable—fraternal interest groups. Since related males can more easily support each other in conflicts if they reside together, patrilocal residence was employed as an index of the presence of fraternal interest groups. The absence of fraternal interest groups was indexed by matrilocal residence, a social structural condition that usually results in the scattering of related males over a large region, making if difficult for them to support each other's interests. In a cross-cultural study using five measures of peacefulness/nonpeacefulness, including the presence or absence of blood feuds, Thoden van Velzen and van Wetering (1960) demonstrated that the presence of fraternal interest groups is responsible for the conflicts that occur within local groups.

Fraternal interest group theory was elaborated and extended by Otterbein and Otterbein to encompass two forms of intergroup violence—feuding (which occurs between kinship groups within a political community) and internal war (which occurs between political communities within the same culture). In two cross-cultural studies, it was shown that the presence of fraternal interest groups predicts feuding and internal war (Otterbein and Otterbein 1965; Otterbein 1968a; 1968c). These studies showed that polygyny, as well as patrilocal residence, may be employed as an index of the presence of fraternal interest groups, since polygyny usually produces a situation in which men have a number of unmarried sons living with them. The feuding study also demonstrated that the level of political integration of the cultures, considered alone, had no influence on the relationship between fraternal interest groups and feuding.

The original formulation of fraternal interest group theory dealt only with competing fraternal interest groups. However, in the elaboration of the theory by Otterbein and Otterbein, the role of officials or political leaders was also taken into account. The results obtained show that if a political community is centralized, and if it engages in warfare, it is unlikely to have feuding even if fraternal interest groups are present. The explanation is offered that officials in centralized political systems have the authority and power to prevent feuding only when their political communities are faced with warfare; in other words, political leaders are reluctant to test the limits of their authority except under demanding circumstances. Presumably, during times of peace, officials will not tax the efficiency of their "governments" by interceding in confrontations between factions within the political community. In times of war, however, in order to present a united front and to staff the military organization, the suppression of feuding and other forms of violence is necessary. For uncentralized political communities, the results obtained suggest that warfare has no influence in suppressing feuding. Indeed, feuding and warfare were found to go hand-in-hand in uncentralized political communities with fraternal interest groups. The results were interpreted to mean that political leaders in these cultures do not have the authority and power under any circumstances, including warfare, to prevent feuding and other forms of violence within their political communities.

ETHNOGRAPHIC STUDIES OF CONFRONTATION

In a field study of the Higi of Nigeria, Keith Otterbein (1968b) described the manner in which the chief and a council of elders would attempt to prevent feuds between fraternal interest groups. The Higi, a tribal people numbering perhaps 120,000, can be considered a "classic" example of a feuding society; social organization is based on extended family households, patrilineages, and patriclans; polygynous marital groups are the norm, and postmarital residence is patrilocal (1969b). Although the Higi chief performs many executive functions (1967, 1968b) too numerous to list here, his authority and power are greatly limited, as the following passage indicates (Otterbein 1968b):

> Blood feuds occur between patrilineages: if a man of one lineage kills a man of another, the dead man's lineage will try to kill the assailant or one of his relatives. . . . When a homicide occurs the chief and elders intervene, and attempt to persuade the victim's relatives to accept compensation. The council meets outside the chief's compound and confers with the relatives of both the killer

and the deceased, after which the amount of compensation, usually in sheep and goats, is determined by the council. If the killing was an accident, the deceased's relatives are less likely to demand revenge, and they may accept a smaller amount of compensation. Successful negotiations sometimes are difficult to achieve because many of the elders belong to the feuding lineages and may not want to accept compensation. . . .

Unfortunately, information on what effect warfare might have had upon the ability of the chief and elders to intervene in feuds was not obtained.

Another cross-cultural study conducted by Keith Otterbein (1979) used both fraternal interest group theory and deterrence theory to predict the frequency of rape. The results obtained show that where there is a major punishment for rape, including capital punishment, exile, and heavy official fines, the frequency of rape is almost always low. However, if fraternal interest groups are absent in cultures with major punishments, the frequency of rape is always low; if fraternal interest groups are present, the frequency of rape can be either high or low. The study also shows that feuding and rape are highly correlated. Although the study does not elaborate upon the reasons why a major punishment for rape should be less effective if fraternal interest groups are present, the previous research by Otterbein and Otterbein (1965) suggests that political leaders, who are the ones to administer major punishments, may meet resistance and interference from a fraternal interest group when one of its members is to be punished for rape. In other words, political leaders may find themselves in confrontations with fraternal interest groups.

Two ethnographic studies of the Metá of western Cameroon, both by Richard G. Dillon, deal directly with fraternal interest group theory (Dillon 1980a) and with capital punishment (Dillon 1980b). In precolonial times, the Metá were an uncentralized or egalitarian society of approximately 15,000. Local groups consisted of the residents of villages of several hundred persons, the members of several unrelated lineages. Each village was governed by a council, presided over by the village chief; the council consisted of "lineage head/notables." In addition to the protection of the village from external threats of sorcery, the responsibilities of this council included the settlement of interlineage disputes within the village (Dillon 1980a: 661). Dillon argues that although fraternal interest groups are present in Metá society, the presence of "conflicting loyalties" results in an "intermediate level of intrasocietal violence" and the "institutionalization of values favoring intrasocietal peace" (Dillon 1980a: 670). In the same study, he points out that dispute settlement sometimes succeeds in uncentralized political systems, even when conflicting loyalties and cross-cutting kinship ties are absent. Dillon mentions two African societies in which members of local groups may execute fellow villagers in order to prevent retaliation from other local groups, and another African society that places a high value on resolving conflicts by negotiation (Dillon 1980a: 659). The execution of a kinsman or a fellow villager cannot be explained, according to Dillon, by fraternal interest group theory; the individual who has transgressed against outsiders should, if fraternal interest group theory is correct, be defended by his fellow kinsmen, with whom he resides.

In the companion article, Dillon uses the Metá as a case study of an egalitarian society in which "ultimate coercive authority was a well-integrated part of the legal machinery" (1980b: 439). The death penalty was usually reserved for habitual witches and thieves. Secrecy characterized the several steps in the decision-making process: A complaint would be brought—often by individuals who were not kin of the offender—to the chief of the offender's village, who in turn would seek the "unanimous assent of the offender's lineage" (1980b: 443) to the execution of the offender. Substantial payments of goats, valuables, and palm wine would be made to the village chief by those bringing the complaint. Once the chief's consent was obtained, the execution could proceed. Usually chosen by the chief for the task would be a member of a lineage recently settled in the area, who would not have kin ties to the offender, i.e., the object of the proposed execution. The executioner, "dressed in a hood of raffia cloth and carrying a . . . soot-blackened club, attempted to surprise the victim, and either kill or subdue him. . . . If the victim had been killed, his corpse was cast into the bush, while if the offender had merely been captured, he was sold by a slave dealer, with the proceeds being turned over to the notables and village chief" (1980b: 445).

Fraternal interest groups, however, were an important factor in Metá legal life. They might not give consent for the execution, and, even having given consent, they might renege if the executioners failed to perform the killing secretly from ambush. "Interlineage fighting broke out in one case in which the executioners are said to have gone undisguised to spear their victim in a public market"

(1980b: 449). Moreover, the "self-help" killing of a thief, or simply the capturing and torturing of the thief, were unusual occurrences: "The fear of violent reprisals by an offender's agnates ordinarily precluded their use" (1980b: 446). Nevertheless, Dillon concludes "that many factors worked together to make capital punishment possible within the egalitarian political order of the Metá," including "distributive" authority, secrecy, and the use of stranger-executioners (1980b: 450). Dillon concludes that, theoretically, the process of ultimate coercive authority "simultaneously functioned to preserve a precarious balance of power among mutually opposed descent groups in an uncentralized society" (1980b: 450). However, the data presented by Dillon can also be interpreted as leading to a different conclusion.

Both of Dillon's studies clearly show the role of political leaders and fraternal interest groups in an uncentralized political system. Not only are the fraternal interest groups seen as being pitted against each other but they are also seen as making use of political leaders to further their own ends. In turn, the political leaders, who are rewarded for their efforts, align themselves periodically with the interests of first one, then another fraternal interest group; thus they may tip the balance in favor of one of the groups. In this manner, political leaders may find themselves in confrontation with fraternal interest groups. Clearly, for the Metá, a strong fraternal interest group can resist the attempt of political leaders to have a member of the group executed. This interpretation differs from Dillon's theoretical conclusion, which views capital punishment as preserving a balance of power in Metá society. Confrontation theory, as set forth below, argues that imbalance may exist and that the entry of political leaders into disputes between fraternal interest groups may create further imbalance, since it is the weaker—not the stronger—fraternal interest group that may be forced to give up a member to the executioner.

In an analysis of legal liability in African tribal societies, Sally Falk Moore (1978) describes the conditions under which a corporate group, such as a fraternal interest group, will either expel or execute one of its own members. The analysis begins with a discussion of group confrontations and the principle of expanding dispute. Simply put, in societies whose legal systems are largely based upon self-help, it is necessary for an individual engaged in a dispute to have the backing of his corporate group; indeed, the dispute does not expand without this backing. Thus, conflicts in these societies are a matter of group, rather than individual, confrontation (Moore

1978: 99–111). Although no mention is made of fraternal interest group theory, Moore's discussion up to this point parallels the theory set forth by Thoden van Velzen and van Wetering (1960). But Moore's theory of legal liability goes further than theirs. Collective obligations exist in situations of self-help that involve expanding disputes: "where every member of a corporate group has the power to commit it in this way to a collective liability a corollary rule always exists whereby the corporation may discipline, expel or yield up to enemies members who abuse this power or whom the corporation does not choose to support in the situation in which he has placed them" (Moore 1978: 121, italics in original omitted). In other words, those individuals who endanger the assets or lives of fellow members of their corporate group are likely to be expelled or executed. "Again and again in the literature, where expulsion is mentioned, or execution by one's own group, it is the gross violator or recidivist who is mentioned" (1978: 123).

A case study of the Montenegrins of the Balkans elaborates upon Moore's analysis. Like the Higi and the Metá, the Montenegrins are a patrilineal, patrilocal tribal people who engage in blood feuding. In an aptly titled paper, "Execution within the Clan as an Extreme Form of Ostracism," Christopher Boehm (1985) reports that a Montenegrin clan might not only repudiate a troublesome clansman—thereby denying him clan protection and exonerating the clan from liability for any killings he might perform—but might even execute such a person. Boehm argues that "the execution within the clan . . . provides the collectivity a means of eliminating two kinds of threat. One is a threat to its collective reputation, and in feuding societies local groups often are rivalrous in this matter. The other threat is that of a feud which will be very costly in blood, time, wealth and psychological stress" (1985: 316). And he argues that "in the case of clan execution . . . fear of consequences from other groups spurs the ostracizers to the extreme of homicidal sanctioning" (1985: 318).

Moore's analysis, as well as Boehm's case study, could go further, however. Two important factors are omitted: First, the relative strength or weakness of the corporate groups is not considered. Dillon's studies of the Metá make it clear that the relative strength or weakness of a fraternal interest group influences whether the group executes or turns over to political leaders or a rival kinship group one of its members. A weak fraternal interest group will be forced to give up a member, while a strong group will not. Here seems to lie the reason why fraternal interest groups do not always defend a fellow kinsman. Second, the role of political leaders in group confrontations is not considered. Again Dillon's study of the Metá shows the role of the chief in carrying out executions. In performing this task, the chief is likely to become involved in confrontations with fraternal interest groups.

The following example, taken from the now famous warring Yanomamö of Venezuela, illustrates what can occur when the fraternal interest groups in a village are matched in size, and dual political leadership exists (Chagnon 1979: 394):

> The dissolution of a marriage where both spouses represent major political factions of the village has more political consequences than the dissolution of marriage where only one spouse comes from a politically significant group. An example illustrates the point. Several years ago in Village 18, the wife of one of the village headmen began having a sexual affair with another man. She came from the other large lineage in the village, and her brother, also one of the village headmen, attempted to persuade her to stop the affair. The two headmen were brothers-in-law and had exchanged sisters in marriage. The woman in question refused to follow her brother's advice, so he killed her with an ax. The recalcitrant woman's brother acted in such a way as to demonstrate to his brother-in-law that he considered the marriage alliance between them and their respective groups of kin to be more important than the life of his sister. The two men were the most important leaders in the village and the fount of the village's solidarity and cohesion and there was, therefore, considerable political pressure on them to keep these bonds strong.

Although a variation on the "typical" situation in which confrontation theory is usually seen to operate, this example clearly supports confrontation theory. The headmen—husband and brother of the woman—were in agreement that she must die for her sexual offense. And the reason is clear: the political stability of the village was threatened.[1]

POLITICAL LEADERS IN CONFRONTATION

Confrontation theory posits that a political leader will be on occasion in conflict with segments of the political community. The conflict arises through the attempts of the political leader and his aides and supporters to control those persons who have committed crimes that threaten the structure of the political community, particularly violent crimes, such as homicide, and sexual offenses. As described above, if a conflict develops between individuals who are members of different fraternal interest groups, group confrontation arises. Since the source of the conflict is often an act that most members of the political community deem to be a crime, the political leader has a reason for becoming involved. If a party to the conflict can be identified as the culprit, the political leader is likely to seek the punishment of this individual. He may also wish to prevent the conflict from being escalated by the contending fraternal interest groups. The political leader and his aides and supporters, in attempting either to prevent the conflict from escalating or to apprehend the culprit, are themselves drawn into the conflict. They may choose to intervene, or they may be requested to do so by one of the contending interest groups, as was the case with the Metá.

When a political leader becomes involved in confrontations with fraternal interest groups, therefore, a three-party situation develops, with the political leader aligning with one of the fraternal interest groups. (In another conflict situation, at a different time, the political leader may align with the other fraternal interest group.) The intercession of the political leader may tip the balance, if a balance has ever existed, in favor of one of the fraternal interest groups. This may force a termination of the conflict or lead to the punishment of the culprit. It also may not do either. A strong fraternal interest group may be able to resist the united forces of the political leader and the rival fraternal interest group. In such a case, the strong fraternal interest group may be asked to deal with its own member; if it does not exile or execute the culprit, the political leader can do nothing more. A weak fraternal interest group may be pressured to turn the culprit over to the political leader or to the aggrieved party for punishment, which often means execution.

The presence of a council of elders, probably representing rival fraternal interest groups if such groups are found within the political community, gives formal institutional backing for the decisions of the political leader. A council may be a major source of supporters for the political leader. The presence on the council of representatives from rival interest groups may make it difficult for the council to reach a consensus, but if a consensus *is* reached, then it is likely that the conflict can be terminated or the culprit punished. Thus councils make the task of governing easier for political leaders. If there are no fraternal interest groups, and hence little likelihood of feuding, a political leader and a council of elders do not have as many serious disputes to settle, nor is it as difficult for them to punish wrongdoers.[2] On the other hand, if fraternal interest groups and feuding are present, the tasks of political leader and council are rendered more difficult.[3]

TYPES OF TRIBAL SOCIETIES

Cultures can be classified in terms of whether or not they have councils of elders and fraternal interest groups. These two dimensions can be used to construct a typology: the presence or absence of councils of elders and the presence or absence of fraternal interest groups. If older, important men within the political community are found on occasion to meet, and if one of these men is the political leader, the culture is classified as having a council of elders. Feuding, rather than fraternal interest groups, was used as the other dimension, since the data for cultures in this study on homicide and feuding are more complete than the data on social organization and residence patterns.

		Feuding	
		Absent	**Present**
Council	**Present**	(1)	(2)
of			
Elders	**Absent**	(4)	(3)

The typology generates four categories: (1) council, no feuding (2) council, feuding (3) no council, feuding, and (4) no council, no feuding. The first three categories divide the tribes in the study into three groups; the last category appeared to remain empty, or residual, until it was realized that the bands, usually defined as hunting and gathering societies, are characterized by an absence of both councils and feuding. Bands, thus, complete the fourth cell of the typology; they do not become relevant for confrontation theory, because they have neither councils nor fraternal interest groups.

The three types of tribal society, when used in conjunction with confrontation theory, lead to a set of predictions about the nature of capital punishment for each of the types of tribal societies. If the data presented in Chapter 9 conform to the predictions, confrontation theory is supported. The predictions are specific to the variations in the steps in the legal process pertaining to capital punishment.

(1) *Council, no feuding.* Homicide will be a capital offense. Jails will be present to hold the offender until the council can decide his fate. Torture, either judicial or *supplice,* may be used to extract a confession and to insure that death is painful—there are no fraternal interest groups who could attempt to rescue the offender or prevent the torture. The execution will be public, and the executioner will be the political leader or his agent. A public method of execution, such as decapitation, hanging, or burning, is likely to be used. Again, there are no fraternal interest groups who could prevent the execution. And the reason for the execution will be the disposal of the wrongdoer. The death penalty will have community approval.

(2) *Council, feuding.* Homicide will be a capital offense within fraternal interest groups and in some instances between fraternal interest groups. Feuding, by definition, is not capital punishment. Our cross-cultural study of feuding provided evidence that even warfare will not strengthen the position of political leaders in uncentralized political systems enough to make it possible for them to be able to prevent feuding (Otterbein and Otterbein 1965). However, if a fraternal interest group wants one of its errant members disposed of, it might permit the political leader and council to execute him. The fraternal interest group may also request the execution of a female relative who has engaged in illicit sexual activity that brought a loss of reputation to the group. Jails will be absent, torture will not be used, the execution will be private or secret, and weapons that can be used in an ambush will be the means of execution. The presence of fraternal interest groups who could rescue one of their members precludes the presence of jails, torture, and public executions. Since the political leader and the elders are likely to be fearful of personal retaliation by the fraternal interest group, they will not carry out the execution, even though the council decided in favor of the death penalty. Instead, the kin of the victim will do the executing, with the concurrence of the kin of the offender. Persons from outside the political community may also be employed for this purpose. Disposal of the wrongdoer will be the reason for the execution.

(3) *No council, feuding.* Without a council to attempt to mediate feuds, it is likely that all intergroup homicides will become part of the vengeance system; that is, all killings are likely to result in blood feuds. However, sexual offenses by women will be treated as capital crimes by their male kinsmen. Jails and torture will, of course, be absent. The kin of the offender will both decide upon the execution and also carry it out, usually in secret, with weapons. As in the case with the other types of tribal societies, the reason for the execution is the disposal of the wrongdoer.

CHAPTER 8

Political Legitimacy Theory: Capital Punishment in Chiefdoms and States

THE DEVELOPMENT OF THE STATE

Political legitimacy theory argues that emerging or recently formed states use a wide range of cruel and repressive sanctions, including torture and capital punishment, to subjugate and control the population. After control is obtained, repressive sanctions are no longer needed; the governing body can rely upon consensus for social regulation. A recent article by Steven Spitzer (1979) describes and critiques four theories or hypotheses that relate punishment to social change or developing political complexity. One of the hypotheses is referred to by Spitzer as "The Political Legitimacy Hypothesis." (Spitzer's summary of the theory is presented below.) Only two studies were discovered, one by Yehudi A. Cohen (1969) and the other by Spitzer (1975), that test the theory. These two tests of the theory are both cross-cultural studies, which use samples of "primitive" societies; results of both studies support the theory.

Cohen's study (1969) explicitly tests political legitimacy theory by relating newly-formed states to the use of capital punishment for sexual crimes. He does not, however, deal with nonsexual crimes, the number of crimes for which capital punishment is used, or the means by which capital punishment is carried out. Three stages in the development of statehood are delineated: (1) inchoate incorporative states, (2) successful incorporative states, and (3) expropriated states. "Incorporative nations are societies that have been united by groups who are geographically contiguous and who are at approximately the same level of cultural development" (1969: 659). "An inchoate incorporative state is one that has not yet completely subverted local sources of solidarity, allegiance, and authority," while "a successful incorporative state is one that has secured the transfer of loyalty and the exercise of authority from local nexuses to the state" (1969: 661). "An expropriated nation is a formerly stateless or state society governed by a state organization imposed by force by another state at a much more advanced level of cultural development" (1969: 660). Using this developmental sequence, Cohen (1969: 662) hypothesizes that "nations characterized by inchoate incorporative states exhibit a unique profile in the regulation of sexual relationships. They adopt laws imposing capital punishment for adultery, incest, and the violation of celibacy." Although his tables do not distinguish between inchoate and successful incorporative states, his data show that incorporative states differ from both expropriated states and stateless societies in that they almost exclusively prescribe capital punishment for the three sex crimes listed (1969: 663–664). An excellent case study utilizing Cohen's theory is Donald Kurtz's "The Legitimation of the Aztec State" (1978). He describes the use of terror and capital punishment by Aztec rulers when the state was at the inchoate incorporative stage of development (1978: 179, 183–184, 186).

Spitzer's study (1975), although designed to test Durkheim's theory of penal evolution, arrived at results that support political legitimacy theory. In his later review article, Spitzer states (1979: 213): "This investigation developed evidence to suggest that the severity of punishment does not decrease as societies grow more concentrated and complex [Durkheim's theory] and that, to the contrary, greater punitiveness seems to be associated with higher levels of structural differentiation." More specifically, he found that ". . . the relationship between punitive intensity and social development is actually curvilinear—in the sense that sanctions are lenient in simple egalitarian (reciprocal) societies, severe in non-market (redistributive) complex societies, and lenient in established market societies . . ." (Spitzer 1975: 633). The explanation for this relationship is to be found in political legitimacy theory: "If punishment is instrumental in consolidating a particular system of domination, then we can explain why greater concentration and complexity lead to harsher and more extensive punitive controls. This would seem to be particularly true in societies where the development of political integration has just begun" (Spitzer 1975: 632). In the review article, Spitzer describes a limitation of the theory (1979: 220–221): "In contradistinction to the political legitimacy hypothesis, . . . ideological and economic controls become far more important than political controls when certain types of pre-industrial states are first attempting to establish effective rule. In situations where local officials . . . must be counted on to support the interests and objectives of the state, coercion may be tried. But in the absence of fine-grained political control and penetration by the state, it was usually far easier to rely on ideological and economic co-optation of local rulers than to undertake a thoroughgoing 'reign of terror.' "

Ibn Khaldūn, a fourteenth-century Arab historian (1332–1406), explained the emergence of statehood with a fully-developed theory of political legitimacy. He delineated three stages in the evolution of a state, which correspond approximately to three forty-year generations. The first stage, when rulers are consolidating power, is characterized by despotism—the use by the political leader of torture and cruel forms of capital punishment to intimidate the controlled population. At this stage, the rulers rely on a strong military to secure the obedience of their subjects. During the second stage, despotism is no longer needed to control the subject people; the ruler is less dependent on the military. This stage, in contrast to the first, is marked by the development of a civilian bureaucracy devoted to collecting taxes and administering justice. Well-established states do not need to employ cruel forms of capital punishment. In the third stage, power becomes concentrated, luxury expands, and docility develops. The state is no longer able to defend itself from attack or prevent internal uprisings. Despotism is no longer available as a means for controlling the population (Ibn Khaldūn 1950: 109–126).[1]

CASE STUDIES OF CAPITAL PUNISHMENT
IN DEVELOPING STATES

Two case studies of capital punishment, one focusing on France (Foucault 1977), the other on England (Hay 1975), provide us with a brief comparative study, which gives collaborative evidence for political legitimacy theory. For eighteenth-century France, Michel Foucault describes in great detail *supplice* (penal torture), judicial torture, and the various forms of capital punishment that were used by the monarch to demonstrate his power and importance (1977: 3–71). The rationale provided by the king's advisors for such practices is also described by Foucault in his study of the evolution of the French penal system from the eighteenth century. The English penal system for the same period is described by Douglas Hay as having been more benign, although capital punishment was prescribed for a great many crimes. The use of the death penalty declined throughout the eighteenth century in England. The impression given by these two studies is that England was one to two centuries ahead of France in reducing the use of the death penalty. Political legitimacy theory provides one explanation: The English state was of greater age than the French nation. By the reign of Henry II (1154–1189), England was a well-administered kingdom, with the English common law dating from that reign (Churchill 1956: 199–225); certainly it was by the time of Elizabeth I (1558–1603). Political stability did not arise in France until the reign of Louis XIV (1643–1715), more than a hundred years later. This comparison of England and France, while certainly not conclusive support for the theory, strongly suggests that a larger-scale comparison might provide evidence for political legitimacy theory.

Another case study dealing with capital punishment also provides support for political legitimacy theory (Harris 1974: 155–203). During the period in which Rome ruled Palestine, the colonial administration and the Roman army were constantly involved in attempting to suppress guerrilla warfare and mass uprisings. Many bandits and guerrilla leaders were crucified. Marvin Harris argues that Jesus's ministry occurred during a peak period of fighting, and that "Jesus himself died a victim of the Roman attempt to destroy the military-messianic consciousness of the Jewish revolutionaries" (1974: 161). Jesus was put to death by Pontius Pilate for inciting uprisings against the Romans and the puppet government they had installed. "To the Romans, Jesus was just another subversive who deserved the same fate as all the other rabble-rousing bandits and

revolutionaries who kept crawling out of the desert" (1974: 192).
The Roman legions finally prevailed in 71 A.D., putting an end to the
more than century-long military-messianic struggle of the Jewish
people. The despotic state became firmly established.

THE POLITICAL LEGITIMACY HYPOTHESIS

Spitzer's summary of "The Political Legitimacy Hypothesis," as
taken from his review, is as follows (1979: 209–210):

> Since effective pacification and management of domestic popula-
> tions will always depend on both political and ideological control
> over the masses, this perspective suggests the formulation of a
> three stage model. Before the development of either political or
> ideological hegemony by the state, social regulation tends to be
> restitutive in character, locally defined, and rooted in the principles
> of reconciliation. However, once states begin to form and arrogate
> power for their own purposes, they must establish repressive
> controls to achieve their ends. Repression is necessary under these
> circumstances because the state must nullify allegiances to local
> sources of authority (i.e., the community, local leaders, kinship
> groups) and establish itself as the single source of legitimate
> authority and power. As long as domestic populations remain
> committed to the "old ways of life," harsh controls are necessary to
> overcome the centrifugal pressures of traditional institutions and
> effectively discipline the masses.
>
> Yet, the coupling of political centralization and repression need
> not continue indefinitely. As soon as the state has achieved a more
> stable basis for its power and established mechanisms to penetrate
> the masses and inculcated the "proper" beliefs, repressive measures
> can be dropped in favor of more sophisticated incentives and
> disincentives. Once the "crisis of state legitimacy" has been
> overcome, it is possible to return to more subtle and structurally
> integrated forms of social regulation. Thus, instead of presenting a
> unilinear theory of punitive evolution in either a restitutive or
> repressive direction, this third perspective develops a curvilinear
> model: stateless societies are regulated through a complex of
> emergent and consensus-based restitutive controls; pristine states,
> precisely because they lack legitimacy, must develop and impose
> harsh, crude, and highly visible forms of repressive sanctions;
> developed states, having successfully "re-invented" consensus,
> can achieve social regulation through a combination of civil law
> and relatively mild forms of "calculated" repression.

Some elaboration of Spitzer's summary is appropriate. Since stateless societies do not form a homogeneous group, it is worth considering whether any particular type of stateless or uncentralized political community might immediately precede the development of the despotic state (inchoate incorporative nation or pristine state). A view commonly accepted, and accepted here, is that chiefdoms are a stage between tribal society and statehood. Chiefdoms have been defined by the presence of economic redistribution and the absence of a government with the legitimate use of force (Service 1962: 143–177; Otterbein 1970/85: 18; Carneiro 1981). Descriptions of chiefdoms strongly suggest that the chief, who is a political leader with formal limited power (Otterbein 1977: 130), often strives to gain power by surrounding himself with armed followers who will do his bidding. Chiefs sometimes appear, as in the Trobriand Islands (see Chapter 4, p. 24), to be petty despots. Chiefdoms, thus, may be a stage preceding the development of the despotic state.

Once the despotic state develops into a mature[2] state (successful incorporative nation or developed state), it may seek to conquer neighboring peoples who are culturally different. If the conquest is successful, the political community becomes a culturally heterogeneous state (Otterbein 1977: 126), and the conquered peoples become dependent native peoples (Otterbein 1977: 19) or, in Cohen's term, expropriated states (1969: 660).

TYPES OF CENTRALIZED POLITICAL SYSTEMS

Despotic states were distinguished from mature states in this study largely by using the criterion of torture. If the ethnographic data make it clear that torture was used to obtain confessions and/or to make death more painful, the culture was classified as a despotic state. On the other hand, if few crimes (four or less) led to execution, if there were few (two or less) means of excuting, and if there were no data describing torture, the culture was classified as a mature state. Application of these criteria permitted dividing the twelve states in this study into two groups: mature states, with five examples, and despotic states, with seven examples.[3]

Political legitimacy theory argues that newly-formed or inchoate incorporative states, to use Cohen's term, struggle to obtain control of the population through the use of torture and capital punishment. Once control is obtained, torture is no longer needed, and fewer crimes are considered to be capital offenses. Inherent in the theory is a time dimension. Also implied is the assumption that development from despotic state to mature state proceeds at a uniform rate—a rate made explicit in Ibn Khaldūn's statement of the theory (1950). Indeed, the following hypothesis, relating chronological age to types of states, can be derived from the above theory: The newer a state is, the more likely it is to be a despotic state; and, conversely, the older a state is, the more likely it is to be a mature state. This hypothesis can be tested by measuring the chronological age of each state at the time of the ethnographic description. The length of time that a state has existed can be obtained by subtracting the year in which the state was formed, as closely as it can be determined, from the year to which the ethnographic reports pertain. This has been done for the twelve states in this study; the data and the hypothesis test are found in Table 6. Support is found for the hypothesis. All the mature states are over two hundred years old, and five of the despotic states are under two hundred years old. The phi coefficient for this relationship is .71, and it is significant at the .05 level, using Fisher's Exact Test. Not only does the test of the hypothesis give credence to political legitimacy theory but it also provides validation for distinguishing between despotic and mature states. There are two deviant cases—the Ganda and the Koreans failed to develop from despotic to mature state after approximately five centuries as states. No suitable explanation has been found to account for why Korea failed to develop into a mature state in nearly five hundred years.

For the Ganda, however, there is evidence that the influence of both Christianity and Islam may have had a destabilizing effect upon what had been a stable African kingdom (Claessen 1979: 191). The extent of instability can be gauged from the fact that the king of Buganda maintained fully supplied canoes on Lake Victoria in case he had to flee his capital in haste (Murdock 1934: 525). Since the Ganda are the most despotic state in the sample, with eight methods of execution (see Chapter 4, p. 32), it may prove instructive to examine the extent to which a regime will go in order to create terror in subordinates and subjugated peoples. The following two passages are only a sample of the many accounts that exist of the cruel forms of execution employed by the king of Ganda. The explorer Speke, in Uganda in 1862, was frequently in the king's presence when executions were ordered. He writes (1864: 350):

> . . . the king instantly sentenced both to death, to prevent the occurrence of such impropriety again; and, to make the example more severe, decreed that their lives should not be taken at once,

TABLE 6

RELATIONSHIP BETWEEN TYPE OF STATE AND LENGTH OF TIME THAT THE APPARATUS OF STATEHOOD HAS BEEN FUNCTIONING

TYPE OF STATE	DATE OF STATE FORMATION	TIME OF FIELD REPORT	AGE OF AGE OF STATE
Despotic			
1. Ashanti	1800	1900	100
2. Azande	1770	1910	140
3. Cuna	1520	1680	160
4. Ganda	1400	1870	470
5. Hausa	1820	1950	130
6. Korea	1392	1890	498
7. Serbs	1830	1900	70
Mature			
1. Amhara	1270	1525	255
2. Bemba	1730	1930	200
3. Kanuri	1100	1950	850
4. Lozi	1600	1900	300
5. Wolof	1400	1940	540

AGE OF STATE

TYPE OF STATE	UNDER 200 YEARS	OVER 200 YEARS	
Despotic	5	2	7
Mature	0	5	5
	5	7	12

$\emptyset = 0.71$ Fisher's Exact Test, $p < .05$

but, being fed to preserve life as long as possible, they were to be dismembered bit by bit, as rations for the vultures, every day, until life was extinct. The dismayed criminals, struggling to be heard, in utter despair, were dragged away boisterously in the most barbarous manner, to the drowning music of the milele and drums.

The king himself might also perform the killing (Speke 1864: 361):

> Today occurred a brilliant instance of the capricious restlessness
> and self-willedness of this despotic king. . . . He had just, it
> seems, mingled a little business with pleasure; for noticing, as he
> passed, a woman tied by the hands to be punished for some
> offense, the nature of which I did not learn, he took the
> executioner's duty on himself, fired at her, and killed her outright.

Chiefdoms, although a separate type of sociopolitical system in Service's classic scheme, are so uncommon that it is difficult to generalize about them in a cross-cultural study; in this study, there are only three examples of chiefdoms.[4] In some aspects, these chiefdoms resemble despotic states, but they are not states. Since chiefdoms may represent a stage preceding the development of the state, they will be grouped with the despotic states when characteristics are predicted (see below). However, for analyses that contrast centralized and uncentralized political systems, chiefdoms will be grouped with all states.

Dependent native peoples come into existence when so-called primitive peoples, whether or not they are at the state level of political complexity, are incorporated into the political system of a conquering state (Otterbein 1977: 19). Five of the cultures can be so classified. Although these cultures are incorporated into mature states, it is best to treat them as a separate category in analyses for two reasons: First, each culture is only a component of a state, and the ethnographic materials pertain to the culture, rather than to the state. Second, to treat an incorporating state as the unit of study, instead of the sample society, would violate sampling procedures. Nevertheless, dependent native peoples will be grouped with mature states when predicting the characteristics of the mature state. For analyses that contrast centralized and uncentralized political systems, the five dependent native peoples will be grouped with chiefdoms and all states; thus, for some analyses, the category of centralized political systems includes despotic states, mature states, chiefdoms, and dependent native peoples.

Political legitimacy theory leads to the following set of predictions for the two major types of centralized political systems: (1) despotic states (including chiefdoms) and (2) mature states (including dependent native peoples). Preliminary support for the theory stems from the finding that type of state is correlated with the length of time that the state has been a state; that is, mature states have been in existence as states for longer periods than have most despotic states (see Table 6). If the data presented in Chapter 9 conform to the predictions, further support for political legitimacy theory is obtained. The predictions are specific to the variations in the steps in the legal process pertaining to capital punishment.

(1) *Despotic states (including chiefdoms)*. Many crimes will be capital offenses, including treason and sexual transgressions. Jails will be present to hold the offender until the political leader decides his fate. Judicial torture and *supplice* will be used to obtain a confession and to insure a painful death.[5] The execution will be public, and the executioner will be the political leader or his agent. A large variety of methods of applying the death penalty will be used. The major reason for the execution will be to show the power of the king. The members of the political community will not accept capital punishment as an appropriate practice.

(2) *Mature states (including dependent native peoples)*. There will be few capital crimes. Jails will be present, but judicial torture will not be used. The political leader will decide the offender's fate, and the executioner will be the political leader or his agent. Although the execution will be public, *supplice* will not be used, and only a few means of causing death will be employed. The reason for the execution will be the disposal of the wrongdoer; and capital punishment will be deemed appropriate by members of the political community.[6]

These, then, are the clusterings of culture traits that, it is anticipated, will accompany each of the two major types of centralized political systems. If all or most of the expected traits are found to be associated with the types, then political legitimacy theory is supported.

PART IV

Analyses and Conclusions

CHAPTER 9

Capital Punishment and Political Systems: Analyses

THE TYPOLOGY OF POLITICAL SYSTEMS

Eight types of political systems have been delineated for this study. The 51 cultures with capital punishment are listed by type of political system in Table 7. Table 8 shows the distribution of political systems by major geographic region. Although the sampling procedure assured that the cultures would be uniformly distributed over the globe, there was no way of predicting whether the types of political systems would, by chance, cluster geographically. They do not cluster; no more than 3 cultures representing a single political type are found in any one geographic region. Except for chiefdoms, which are concentrated in Oceania, each political type is represented in two or more regions. This worldwide distribution of political systems suggests that the typology that has been developed will be useful in comparing and analyzing diverse cultures. The typology is culture-free, and therefore it can be used as a variable in cross-cultural analyses.

TABLE 7

CULTURES BY TYPE OF POLITICAL SYSTEM

MATURE STATE	DEPENDENT NATIVE PEOPLES	DESPOTIC STATE	CHIEFDOM	BANDS
Amhara	Bahia Brazilians	Ashanti	Lau	Aranda
Bemba	Garo	Azande	Trobriands	Klamath
Kanuri	Kurd	Cuna	Truk	Lapps
Lozi	Sinhalese	Ganda		Ojibwa
Wolof	Tzeltal	Hausa		Ona
		Korea		Pgymies
		Serbs		

COUNCIL, FEUDING NOT PRESENT	COUNCIL, FEUDING PRESENT	NO COUNCIL, FEUDING PRESENT
Bush Negroes	Blackfoot	Guarani
Cagaba	Chukchee	Ifugao
Dogon	Masai	Kapauku
Hopi	Somali	Senussi
Iban	Tiv	Tucano
Iroquois	Tlingit	Yanoama
Khasi	Toradja	
Santal	Yakut	
Shluh		
Tarahumara		
Tikopia		

TABLE 8

DISTRIBUTION OF POLITICAL SYSTEMS BY MAJOR GEOGRAPHIC REGION

POLITICAL SYSTEM	NORTH AMERICA	SOUTH AMERICA	AFRICA	MEDITERRANEAN	EURASIA	OCEANIA	TOTAL
Mature state	—	—	2	3	—	—	5
Dependent Native Peoples	1	1	—	1	2	—	5
Despotic State	—	1	3	1	2	—	7
Chiefdom	—	—	—	—	—	3	3
Council/ No Feuding	3	2	1	1	2	2	11
Council/ Feuding	2	—	2	1	2	1	8
No Council/ Feuding	—	3	—	1	—	2	6
Band	2	1	1	—	1	1	6
TOTAL	8	8	9	8	9	9	51

87

The three theories presented in Chapters 6, 7, and 8 are not competing theories, but are separate theories, which pertain to political systems at different levels of sociopolitical complexity. In outline form, the correspondences between theories and types of political systems are the following:

Theories	Types of Political Systems
Political Legitimacy Theory	Mature state Dependent native peoples Despotic state Chiefdom
Confrontation Theory (Tribe)	Council, feuding not present Council, feuding present No council, feuding present
Group Survival Theory	Bands

Dependent native peoples and chiefdoms are listed above with the mature and despotic states, because of their affinities with states and because they can be classified along with states as centralized political systems.

In this chapter, type of political system will be treated as a variable and as a set of distinct types. Each step in the legal process, as detailed in Chapter 4, will be related to political type. Thus it will be possible to examine the characteristics of each political type for each step in the legal process relating to capital punishment. The separate theories describe characteristics of the political types to which they pertain. If the actual characteristics correspond to these anticipated characteristics, as set forth by the separate theories, then the compatibility of the data with the expected characteristics supports the theories.

RELATIONSHIP OF TYPE OF POLITICAL SYSTEM TO THE LEGAL PROCESS

In the analyses that follow, type of political system is used as the independent variable, and the steps in the legal process are used as the dependent variables. Each step of the process is examined in terms of how it varies from one political type to another. Two types of tables are employed: (1) If multiple categories or scores on the dependent variable are possible for each culture, a percentage table is produced. Each column of the table provides the percentage of cultures for each political type that have that particular score on the variable. Percentages, rather than frequencies, must be used in order to make the information within a single table comparable. (2) If only one score on the dependent variable is possible, an N-x-N contingency table is produced. Frequencies, not percentages, are used in such tables. Since a stratified probability sample was used, it is appropriate to compute correlation coefficients and tests of significance.

The political systems vary in terms of the crimes that are treated as capital offenses (see Table 9). All states, both mature and despotic, execute for homicide. A majority of states use the death penalty for stealing (80 percent and 86 percent) and for witchcraft (60 percent and 57 percent). Despotic states and chiefdoms find treason (86 percent and 100 percent) and sexual offenses (71 percent and 67 percent) to be capital crimes. The latter finding is consistent with the result obtained by Cohen (1969: 669), to the effect that inchoate incorporative states execute for sexual offenses. The close similarity of chiefdoms to despotic states, particularly in terms of treason, suggests that chiefdoms can be viewed as a preliminary stage before the emergence of the despotic state. Such a conclusion must be tentative, however, since there are only three chiefdoms in this study, and they are concentrated in Oceania.

Tribal-level political communities with councils, whether feuding is present or not, frequently regard homicide as a capital offense (75 percent and 64 percent). On the other hand, political communities without councils, including bands, regard witchcraft as a serious crime (67 percent and 83 percent). Political communities with feuding, as well as despotic states and chiefdoms, are likely to execute for sexual offenses (63 percent and 67 percent). This is in contrast to Cohen's finding that stateless societies were not likely to employ the death penalty for sexual offenses; his results appear to hold only for inchoate incorporative states. The fact that political communities with feuding have fraternal interest groups, which jealously guard the chastity and honor of their women, may explain the strong relationship between feuding and the death penalty for sexual offenses. The integrity of the group is maintained by executing female members whose sexual behavior threatens the reputation of the kinship group.

TABLE 9

CAPITAL CRIMES (In Percentages Per Type Of Political System)

POLITICAL SYSTEM	NUMBER	TREASON	ASSASSINATION	HOMICIDE	STEALING	WITCHCRAFT	SEXUAL OFFENSES	DESERTION	OTHER
Mature State	5	20(1)	—	100(5)	80(4)	60(3)	20(1)	—	20(1)
Dependent Native Peoples	5	—	—	40(2)	20(1)	20(1)	40(2)	—	60(3)
Despotic State	7	86(6)	14(1)	100(7)	86(6)	57(4)	71(5)	14(1)	57(4)
Chiefdom	3	100(3)	—	33(1)	33(1)	33(1)	67(2)	—	33(1)
Council/ No Feuding	11	27(3)	—	64(7)	64(7)	55(6)	45(5)	—	27(3)
Council/ Feuding	8	13(1)	—	75(6)	38(3)	25(2)	63(5)	13(1)	25(2)
No Council/ Feuding	6	—	17(1)	33(2)	17(1)	67(4)	67(4)	—	33(2)
Band	6	—	—	33(2)	50(3)	83(5)	33(2)	—	33(2)
TOTAL	51	(14)	(2)	(32)	(26)	(26)	(26)	(2)	(18)

TABLE 10

NUMBER OF CAPITAL CRIMES

POLITICAL SYSTEM	NUMBER	1	2	3	4	5	6	7	8
Mature State	5	—	1	2	2	—	—	—	—
Dependent Native Peoples	5	2	2	1	—	—	—	—	—
Despotic State	7	—	—	2	—	2	1	—	2
Chiefdom	3	1	—	1	—	1	—	—	—
Council/No Feuding	11	3	—	4	4	—	—	—	—
Council/Feuding	8	3	1	3	—	—	—	1	—
No Council/Feuding	6	4	—	—	—	1	—	1	—
Band	6	2	—	4	—	—	—	—	—
Total	51	15	4	17	6	4	1	2	2

The bimodal distribution of the number of crimes for which the death penalty is used, as discussed in Chapter 4, cuts across all political types except the despotic states. All despotic states execute for three or more crimes; the other seven types of political systems execute for fewer reasons. The distribution by type of political system is found in Table 10. Although the world may divide into (1) those cultures that reserve capital punishment for the one offense that they regard as a heinous crime and (2) those cultures that believe that capital punishment is an appropriate punishment for any number of crimes, it should be noted that most of the cultures in this study (36 out of 51 cultures) execute for three or fewer crimes. Thus, even though all cultures have capital punishment, most are restrictive in the use they make of the death penalty.

The more complex political systems, as might be expected, have developed means of incarcerating criminals (see Table 11). The types of political systems are grouped in the table to reveal this relationship. The tau-b correlation coefficient of .54 is significant at the .001 level. No major differences occur within the groupings. The table clearly shows, with the one exception of the semi-nomadic, band-level Lapps, that means of permanent incarceration or jails are found only in centralized political systems and in cultures with councils and no feuding. Tribes with councils differ, depending upon whether feuding is present or not. It appears that if feuding is present, jails are not; and if feuding is absent, some form of permanent or temporary incarceration is present. Confrontation theory argues that the presence of fraternal interest groups prevents

TABLE 11

FACILITIES FOR HOLDING PRISONERS

POLITICAL SYSTEM	NONE	TEMPORARY INCARCERATION	PERMANENT INCARCERATION	TOTAL
Centralized	2	1	8	11
Council/No Feuding	1	2	3	6
Tribes with Feuding and Bands	8	2	1	11
Total	11	5	12	28

Cases with no data: 23

tau_b = .54 z = 4.00 $p < .001$

the permanent incarceration, and perhaps even the temporary incarceration, of criminals. Jails not only must keep people in but must also keep people out. It would be difficult for council members and their supporters to keep fraternal interest groups from attacking and rescuing incarcerated kinsmen. Even at the state level of sociopolitical complexity, kin may attempt rescues. The infamous Salem witchcraft trails provide examples (Boyer and Nissenbaum 1974: 3, 33).

Judicial torture is not commonly used (see Table 12). Of the 27 cultures for which there are data, only 8 employ torture to extract

TABLE 12

JUDICIAL TORTURE

POLITICAL SYSTEM	ABSENT	PRESENT	TOTAL
Centralized	3	4	7
Council/No Feuding	4	2	6
Tribes with Feuding and Bands	12	2	14
Total	19	8	27

Cases with no data: 24

tau_c = .37 z = 2.73 $p < .01$

confessions. Of the centralized political systems, only the 4 despotic states for which there are data make use of torture. Only a third of the tribes with councils and no feuding and one-seventh of the tribes with feuding and bands use torture. The tau-c correlation coefficient of .37 is significant at the .01 level. In a small-scale society, a criminal—as well as his behavior—is likely to be well known to most members of the political community; and, hence, the obtaining of involuntary confessions from suspects is not necessary.

Political systems vary in terms of who decides that the criminal is to be executed (see Table 13). The political leaders of all states, both mature and despotic, make the decision; and, rarely will that authority be shared with another possible decision-making group. Of the 12 states for which there are data, only 3 states share that authority: of the mature states, the Kanuri political leaders share with religious practitioners, and the Lozi political leaders share with both the kin of the offender and the kin of the victim. Political leaders of one despotic state, the Serbs, share authority with a council. On the other hand, uncentralized political systems permit a variety of groups to make the decision; all six decision-making groups—political leader, council, kin of offender, religious practitioner, kin of victim, and community—are well represented among the smaller-scale societies. Some variation within this grouping does occur however: In political systems with councils, whether feuding is present or not, councils are likely to decide (50 percent and 63 percent); in political systems without councils—tribes and bands—there is a tendency for the kin of the offender to decide (60 percent and 50 percent).

The social context in which the execution takes place varies with the type of political system (see Table 14a). Mature states and despotic states are likely to have public executions exclusively (100 percent and 67 percent), although the secret setting is maintained as an additional option by some despotic states (33 percent). At the tribal level of sociopolitical complexity, tribes with councils and no feuding have public executions or public and secret executions (71 percent); while tribes with councils and feuding have private or secret executions (50 percent and 25 percent). The same explanation given above for the absence of jails in tribes with councils and feuding applies here; namely, fraternal interest groups could attempt to interfere and perhaps successfully prevent the execution of the kinsman if the execution were public. Political systems

TABLE 13

WHO DECIDES ON EXECUTION (In Percentages Per Type Of Political System)

POLITICAL SYSTEM	NUMBER	NO DATA	BASE NUMBER	POLITICAL LEADER	COUNCIL	KIN OF OFFENDER	RELIGIOUS PRACTITIONER	KIN OF VICTIM	COMMUNITY
Mature State	5	0	5	100(5)	—	20(1)	20(1)	20(1)	—
Dependent Native Peoples	5	1	4	50(2)	25(1)	25(1)	—	—	25(1)
Despotic State	7	0	7	100(7)	14(1)	—	—	—	—
Chiefdom	3	0	3	67(2)	—	—	—	—	67(2)
Council/ No Feuding	11	3	8	38(3)	50(4)	13(1)	25(2)	13(1)	25(2)
Council/ Feuding	8	0	8	13(1)	63(5)	25(2)	13(1)	25(2)	25(2)
No Council/ Feuding	6	1	5	20(1)	—	60(3)	20(1)	20(1)	—
Bands	6	2	4	—	25(1)	50(2)	—	—	50(2)
Total	51	7	44	(21)	(12)	(10)	(5)	(5)	(9)

TABLE 14a

SOCIAL CONTEXT OF EXECUTION (In Percentages Per Type Of Political System)

POLITICAL SYSTEM	NUMBER	NO DATA	BASE NUMBER	PUBLIC	PRIVATE	SECRET	PUBLIC AND SECRET
Mature State	5	4	1	100(1)	—	—	—
Dependent Native Peoples	5	4	1	—	—	100(1)	—
Despotic State	7	1	6	67(4)	—	—	33(2)
Chiefdom	3	1	2	50(1)	—	—	50(1)
Council/ No Feuding	11	4	7	57(4)	14(1)	14(1)	14(1)
Council/ Feuding	8	4	4	25(1)	50(2)	25(1)	—
No Council/ Feuding	6	1	5	40(2)	20(1)	40(2)	—
Bands	6	3	3	—	—	100(3)	—
Total	51	22	29	(13)	(4)	(8)	(4)

95

without councils, including bands, have secret executions (40 percent and 100 percent). Thus centralized political systems are likely to have public executions, and uncentralized political systems without councils are likely to have secret executions. This relationship between the level of political complexity and the extent to which executions are public probably reflects the power of political leaders—the greater power of kings in contrast to that of headmen and chiefs (Otterbein 1977: 130) means that they can publicly carry out the death sentence without interference from the kin of the culprit. Table 14b, which is derived from Table 14a, contrasts centralized and uncentralized political systems; almost all societies with centralized political systems (9 of 10) have public executions, perhaps with secret as well; while more than half of the societies with uncentralized political systems (11 of 19) have exclusively private or secret executions. The phi coefficient for this relationship is .46, and it is significant at the .02 level.

Political systems vary in terms of who carries out the execution (see Table 15). All despotic states and chiefdoms have political leaders or agents of political leaders who carry out the death sentence. The most notable observation that can be made about the information in Table 15 is that all of the five categories of executioners—political leader, kin of victim, kin of offender, self-inflicted, and community—are found in nearly every type of political community. Only judicial suicide is confined to four, or half of the types.[1] In the council, no feuding, type of political system, the political leaders are likely to carry out the execution (57 percent). In the council, with feuding, type of political system, the

TABLE 14b

SOCIAL CONTEXT OF EXECUTION

POLITICAL SYSTEM	PUBLIC, PUBLIC AND SECRET	PRIVATE, SECRET	TOTAL
Centralized	9	1	10
Uncentralized	8	11	19
Total	17	12	29

$\emptyset = .46$ $X^2 = 6.20$ $.01 < p < .02$

TABLE 15

WHO EXECUTES (In Percentages Per Type Of Political System)

POLITICAL SYSTEM	NUMBER	NO DATA	BASE NUMBER	POLITICAL LEADER	KIN OF VICTIM	KIN OF OFFENDER	SELF-INFLICTED	COMMUNITY
Mature State	5	1	4	25(1)	50(2)	25(1)	—	—
Dependent Native Peoples	5	3	2	50(1)	—	100(2)	—	50(1)
Despotic State	7	0	7	100(7)	14(1)	29(2)	14(1)	43(3)
Chiefdom	3	0	3	100(3)	33(1)	—	33(1)	—
Council/ No Feuding	11	4	7	57(4)	43(3)	29(2)	29(2)	29(2)
Council/ Feuding	8	1	7	29(2)	71(5)	29(2)	14(1)	43(3)
No Council/ Feuding	6	1	5	—	40(2)	60(3)	—	20(1)
Band	6	4	2	50(1)	50(1)	50(1)	—	—
Total	51	14	37	(19)	(15)	(13)	(5)	(10)

97

kin of the victim may execute (71 percent), even though they do not make the decision. As pointed out above, councils—if they are present—are likely to make the decision to execute. It appears that even though councils are willing to make the decision, they are unwilling to carry out the execution if fraternal interest groups are present. The actual task is turned over to the kin of the victim, who probably want to see the death penalty enacted. In feud-based political communities, council members might be reluctant to perform executions for fear of embroiling themselves in a feud; that is, the kin of the executed person might decide to take vengeance upon them or their relatives. In the no council, with feuding, type of political system, the kin of the offender may execute (60 percent). In these cultures, the offender who is killed is likely to be a member of the kinship group that is responsible for the execution. In the no council, with feuding, type of political system, the fraternal interest groups are required, it would appear, to play a major role in controlling the deviant or criminal behavior of their members. It has been shown above that witchcraft and sexual offenses are the major reasons for the death penalty in these political systems. Where councils are present, elders assume a larger role in controlling behavior.

Torturing criminals to death is associated with the more complex political systems (see Table 16). Of the 11 centralized political

TABLE 16

TORTURING CRIMINALS TO DEATH

POLITICAL SYSTEM	ABSENT	PRESENT	TOTAL
Centralized	3	8	11
Council/No Feuding	3	3	6
Tribes with Feuding and Bands	15	0	15
Total	21	11	32

Cases with no data: 19

$tau_c = .70$ $z = 5.66$ $p < .001$

systems for which there are data, 6 despotic states, 1 mature state, and 1 chiefdom use *supplice*; 2 chiefdoms and 1 dependent native peoples do not. Political systems with councils and no feuding divide equally on whether or not they torture. And none of the 15 cultures with the simplest political systems torture. The tau-c correlation coefficient of .70 is significant at the .001 level. Thus for *supplice* to occur, a political community seemingly must have developed politically to the point where either a council or a powerful political leader is present, and fraternal interest groups, which might have the ability to prevent the torturing of a kinsman, are either weak or nonexistent.

In a majority of cultures, the death penalty is likely to be carried out with weapons (see Table 17). Although the use of weapons dominates in all political types except mature states and dependent native peoples, various different means are found in all types of political systems. Each of the seven major means of executing delineated in this study—decapitating, drowning, hanging, burning, poisoning, incapacitating, and using weapons—is used by 2 or more of the 7 despotic states. Most cultures, however, use only one or two means (see Table 18): one-half use only one method, while an additional one-quarter use two. Despotic states stand out from all other political types, in that they use from two to eight means of executing. Indeed, only despotic states use four or more means: all other political types use three or less.

Disposal of the wrongdoer is the major reason for capital punishment (see Table 19): 18 cultures out of 26 for which there are data have disposal of the wrongdoer as a reason for using the death penalty. (Eleven cultures have disposal of the wrongdoer as the only reason, and 7 more cultures have disposal as one of two reasons.) Because of the scarcity of data for the centralized political systems, this finding is most apparent for the uncentralized political systems. Revenge is also a reason for capital punishment in less complex societies. Other reasons include showing the power of the king, a reason found only in despotic states.

Finally, the degree of acceptance of capital punishment is widespread: 26 out of 29 cultures for which there are data have populations that favor capital punishment. Because of the nearly universal support for capital punishment a table presenting these data is unnecessary.

TABLE 17

MANNER IN WHICH EXECUTION IS CARRIED OUT (In Percentages, Per Type Of Political System)

POLITICAL SYSTEM	Number	No Data	Base Number	Decapitating	Drowning	Hanging	Burning	Poisoning	Incapacitating	Using Weapons	Other
Mature State	5	2	3	—	—	33(1)	33(1)	33(1)	33(1)	—	33(1)
Dependent Native Peoples	5	2	3	—	—	67(2)	—	—	—	33(1)	33(1)
Despotic State	7	0	7	43(3)	57(4)	71(5)	57(4)	43(3)	29(2)	100(7)	57(4)
Chiefdom	3	0	3	—	—	—	—	—	—	100(3)	33(1)
Council/ No Feuding	11	2	9	—	—	44(4)	22(2)	11(1)	11(1)	44(4)	11(1)
Council/ Feuding	8	1	7	—	43(3)	43(3)	14(1)	—	29(2)	71(5)	—
No Council/ Feuding	6	2	4	—	—	—	—	25(1)	25(1)	50(2)	—
Band	6	2	4	—	—	50(2)	—	—	25(1)	75(3)	25(1)
Total	51	11	40	(3)	(7)	(17)	(8)	(6)	(8)	(25)	(8)

TABLE 18

NUMBER OF WAYS OF EXECUTING

POLITICAL SYSTEM	NUMBER	NO DATA	BASE NUMBER	1	2	3	4	5	6	7	8
Mature State	5	2	3	1	2	—	—	—	—	—	—
Dependent Native Peoples	5	2	3	3	—	—	—	—	—	—	—
Despotic State	7	0	7	—	1	1	2	1	1	—	1
Chiefdom	3	0	3	2	1	—	—	—	—	—	—
Council/ No Feuding	11	2	9	5	4	—	—	—	—	—	—
Council/ Feuding	8	1	7	3	1	3	—	—	—	—	—
No Council/ Feuding	6	2	4	4	—	—	—	—	—	—	—
Bands	6	2	4	2	1	1	—	—	—	—	—
Total	51	11	40	20	10	5	2	1	1	0	1

TABLE 19

REASONS FOR EXECUTION (In Percentages, Per Type Of Political System)

POLITICAL SYSTEM	NUMBER	NO DATA	BASE NUMBER	DISPOSAL OF WRONGDOER	REVENGE	DETERRENCE	OTHER
Mature State	5	5	0	—	—	—	—
Dependent Native Peoples	5	3	2	—	50(1)	—	50(1)
Despotic State	7	3	4	50(2)	—	25(1)	50(2)
Chiefdom	3	2	1	100(1)	100(1)	—	—
Council/ No Feuding	11	5	6	100(6)	33(2)	17(1)	—
Council/ Feuding	8	4	4	75(3)	50(2)	—	—
No Council/ Feuding	6	2	4	75(3)	50(2)	—	—
Band	6	1	5	60(3)	20(1)	20(1)	20(1)
Total	51	25	26	(18)	(9)	(3)	(4)

SUMMARY

The analyses have shown the differences among the eight types of political systems for each step in the legal process associated with capital punishment. The salient characteristics or culture traits for each political type are enumerated below (see Table 20); most of the characteristics are not unique to any one political type. For each type of political system, there is a distinct set or cluster of culture traits; these clusters of traits correspond to many of the predicted characteristics of the political types as set forth in the three theories presented in Chapters 6, 7, and 8.

The centralized political systems, as a group, have centralized capital punishment; political leaders decide upon execution, jails hold criminals, and the executions take place in public. Of the four types of centralized political systems, despotic states are the most distinct type; they execute for many crimes, use judicial torture, use *supplice*, employ many means of executing, and use the death penalty to show the power of the king. Surprisingly there is support for the executions, the Ganda being the only despotic state where there is not public support. Chiefdoms resemble despotic states, in that they execute for treason and sexual offenses, and the political leader or his agent performs the execution. On the other hand, mature states execute for few crimes, do not use judicial torture or *supplice*, and employ only a limited number of means of executing. Dependent native peoples resemble mature states, although paucity of data makes this comparison inconclusive. These clusters of culture traits correspond to the characteristics predicted by political legitimacy theory.

Of the uncentralized political systems, each type of tribe is sufficiently distinct from the other two types to warrant maintaining the typology that was developed for this study. Tribes with councils and no feuding have councils who decide upon execution—the crime usually being homicide—and political leaders who execute. They also have jails. Some of them use judicial torture and *supplice*, and their executions are public. In all of these respects, tribes with councils and no feuding resemble centralized political systems. Tribes with councils and with feuding differ in several respects from tribes with councils and no feuding: In addition to homicide, sexual offenses are capital crimes; there are no jails and no torture; and executions—although decided upon by the council—are conducted in private or in secret by the kin of the victim. Since councils are present in both types, the differences can be attributed to the presence or absence of fraternal interest groups and feuding.

TABLE 20

RELATIONSHIP OF POLITICAL TYPES TO STEPS IN THE LEGAL PROCESS

POLITICAL SYSTEM	Crimes	Number Of Crimes	Jails	Judicial Torture	Who Decides	Social Context	Who Executes	Supplice	Means	Number	Reasons	Public Support
Mature State	Homicide Stealing Witchcraft	Low	Yes	No	Political leader	Public	—	Rare	—	Low	—	Present
Dependent Native Peoples		Low	Yes	No	Political leader	—	—	Rare	—	Low	—	Present
Despotic State	Homicide Stealing Witchcraft Treason Sexual Offenses	High	Yes	Yes	Political leader	Public	Political leader	Yes	Weapons	High	Showing power of king	Present
Chiefdom	Treason Sexual Offenses	Low	Yes	No	Political leader	—	Political leader	Rare	Weapons	Low	—	Present

Council/ No Feuding	Homicide	Low	Yes	Sometimes	Council	Public	Political leader	Sometimes	Weapons	Low	Disposal of wrongdoer	Present
Council/ Feuding	Homicide Sexual Offenses	Low	No	No	Council	Private, or Secret	Kin of victim	No	Weapons	Low	Disposal of wrongdoer	Present
No Council/ Feuding	Witchcraft Sexual Offenses	Low	No	No	Kin of offender	Secret	Kin of offender	No	Weapons	Low	Disposal of wrongdoer	Present
Band	Witchcraft	Low	No	No	Community, Kin of offender	Secret	—	No	Weapons	Low	Disposal of wrongdoer	Present

— = no frequency high enough to warrant inclusion on table

Confrontation theory predicts these differences. Tribes without councils and with feuding differ from the tribes that have both councils and feuding. The absence of councils in political communities with feuding seems to be related to the following culture traits: Witchcraft and sexual offenses are capital crimes, and the kin of the offender both decide on execution and execute the culprit, in secret. Without a council, homicides do not receive legal treatment; they remain part of the feuding or vengeance system of the political community. Capital crimes are offenses that are dealt with by the fraternal interest group to which the culprit belongs; law is shifted from the political community as a whole to its constituent parts.

Bands greatly resemble the tribes without councils and with feuding, although bands by definition do not have fraternal interest groups or feuding. The main difference is that bands view witchcraft and related phenomena as their main capital crime. This concern with sacrilegious acts that are dangerous to the entire band is compatible with group survival theory. The community or kin of an offender decides upon the execution.

Three theories of capital punishment were developed in detail in Chapters 6, 7, and 8; lists of predicted characteristics for the political types associated with each theory were set forth. It was argued that, if the data presented in this chapter conformed to the predictions, support for each theory would be obtained. The data presented here, as summarized in Table 20, do conform to the predictions. Thus, direct support has been obtained for each of the three theories— group survival theory, confrontation theory, and political legitimacy theory.

peoples. The theories are tested by the method of the cross-cultural survey; the data base is a 60-society probability sample taken from the Human Relations Area Files. Support is found for the predictions derived from the theories.

The first theory, group survival theory, argues that any act that is seen by the members of a band as threatening the survival of their group will subject the perpetrator of that act to capital punishment. Findings that support predictions from the theory include: Those offenses that endanger the welfare of the group—incest, sacrilegious acts (such as sorcery, witchcraft, and violations of taboos), and homicide—are capital offenses. The community decides upon the execution. The execution occurs in secret, with weapons.

The second theory, confrontation theory, argues that in tribal society, fraternal interest groups are not only pitted against each other but may also find themselves in confrontation with political leaders. The presence of a council gives backing to the decisions of political leaders, while the presence of fraternal interest groups makes it difficult for such leaders to enforce their decisions. In order to derive predictions, a typology of tribes was developed. Findings that support predictions pertaining to each type include the following: (1) Tribes with councils and no feuding (no fraternal interest groups) view homicide as a capital offense. Jails are present to hold the offender until the council can decide his fate. The execution is public, and the executioner is the political leader or his agent. (2) Tribes with councils and feuding consider homicide to be a capital offense within fraternal interest groups. However, if a fraternal interest group is willing to have one of its errant members disposed of, it may permit the political leader and council to execute him. Jails are absent. Although the council decides in favor of capital punishment, the kin of the victim perform the execution, in secret, with the concurrence of the kin of the offender. (3) Tribes without councils but with feuding do not treat homicides as capital crimes. However, sexual offenses by women are treated as capital crimes by their male kinsmen. The kin of the offender both decide upon the execution and carry it out, usually in secret, with weapons.

The third theory, political legitimacy theory, argues that emerging or recently formed states employ a wide range of cruel and repressive sanctions, including torture and capital punishment, to subjugate and control the population. After control is obtained, repressive sanctions are no longer needed; the governing body can rely upon consensus for social regulation. Two major types of centralized political systems form the basis for different predictions.

Some of the findings that support the predictions include the following: (1) Despotic states, including chiefdoms, have many capital crimes. Jails are present; judicial torture and *supplice* are used to obtain a confession and to insure a painful death. Many different methods of applying the death penalty are used. The major reason for the execution is to show the power of the king. (2) Mature states, including dependent native peoples, have few capital crimes. Jails are present, but judicial torture and *supplice* are not used. Only a few means of causing death are employed. The reason for the execution is the disposal of the wrongdoer.

Theoretically, the strong support that is obtained for the theories permits the conclusion that an adequate explanation for the occurrence of the death penalty and its various forms has been found. Descriptively, the cross-cultural study leads to the conclusion that capital punishment is a central, integral part of every legal and political system. Capital punishment is a universal culture trait. However, capital punishment as a legal process differs among the eight types of political systems that have been analyzed in this study. The study has shown how the efforts of political leaders in different types of political systems to arrogate to themselves the right to execute have made for differences in the manner in which capital punishment has been institutionalized. Capital punishment is the most effective means of physical coercion that is available to political leaders and community members for disposing of criminals who have threatened the community and its members. It is the most extreme form of privileged force, privileged force being one of the three elements, along with official authority and regularity, that make a custom into a law. The death penalty is the ultimate coercive sanction.

Epilogue

All peoples use capital punishment when they believe that it is necessary to dispose of an individual who threatens them and their community. Once executed, the criminal no longer poses a threat to the community. If the members of a political community do not choose to use capital punishment, an alternative must be found to reduce crime. The most popular alternative response seems to be life in prison. This response is not effective; criminals incarcerated for "life" are not in prison for the rest of their lives. They may be pardoned, or released in a few years, or they may escape. Community members know that this is the case.

In a stable, mature state—one that is not at war—crime and the fear of crime are not likely to be major societal concerns, and therefore community members feel no real need for the death penalty; indeed, the political leaders themselves lack the fear that seemingly haunts the leaders of unstable, despotic states. Time alone seemingly can contribute to the stability of a state. This study, however, did not directly explore the basis of political stability. Surely those social science researchers who seek to eliminate capital punishment should pursue this direction. Anything that can be done to reduce crime and the threat of criminal activities will reduce the demand for the death penalty.

One final thought: Activists—those who oppose capital punishment—should work for a stable society. And those who favor capital punishment should do the same. Eliminating capital punishment is probably an unobtainable goal. Statute law may state that there shall be no capital punishment, but if the members of a political community feel that there is a need for the death penalty, the law will be changed, and executions will occur. On the other hand, high rates of capital punishment are also unlikely, at least in the United States and in the other Western industrial nations. Anti-capital-punishment groups should redirect their energies. They, along with the supporters of capital punishment, should work to find more effective means for reducing crime.

Notes

NOTES TO PROLOGUE

1   The term "ultimate coercive sanction" comes from Richard Dillon's case study of Metá capital punishment (1980b); his study is reviewed in Chapter 7.

CHAPTER 1

1   The reasons and the arguments that have been developed to explain why capital punishment has been so little studied closely parallel the reasons I have set forth to explain why anthropologists, as of approximately 1960, were little concerned with the study of warfare (Otterbein 1973:926).

2   While my wife and I were doing fieldwork in Long Bay Cays, Bahamas, in 1968, there was a case of capital punishment—a hanging—in Nassau, the capital city. This event is not described in any of our ethnographic reports, however, because it was not relevant to the particular village where we were working.

3   The particular television program that I watched was PBS's six-part series entitled "Elizabeth R," starring Glenda Jackson.

CHAPTER 2

1   In coding, Naroll's definition of a territorial team was used to distinguish political communities (1964: 286): "A group of people whose membership is defined in terms of occupancy of a common territory and who have an official with the special function of announcing group decisions—a function exercised at least once a year."

CHAPTER 3

1   In 1976, I stated that the HRAF sample was suitable for a "publishable pilot study, using one's own codings" (Otterbein 1976: 111).

2   The students were Mukunda Aryal, Karen McCadden, and JoEllen Ruperto.

3   In this monograph, both correlation coefficients and tests of signifcance are presented, although I have stated elsewhere (Otterbein 1976: 115–116) that tests of significance, or inferential statistics, are not appropriate for the Probability Sample Files, since the sample is a disproportional stratified sample, to which a weighting procedure cannot be satisfactorily applied. Nevertheless, tests of significance are viewed by some researchers as descriptive statistics, as well as inferential statistics, and for this reason they are presented here, along with the strictly descriptive statistics—the correlation coefficients.

4   The students were Christine Eber, Ann Herbert, David Hom, David Kieber, Richard Lewis, Kathryn Schenk, Paul Shackel, Annmarie Stofey, Russell Tulp, and Jennifer Young.

CHAPTER 4

1   The second legal process—jumping from the coconut palm tree—is the classic example. Many anthropologists are familiar with Malinowski's detailed description of the case; he was conducting fieldwork in the community at the time the suicide occurred. Much less familiar are the "henchmen" who execute on behalf of the chief, although Malinowski briefly described such killings in three sources. Hoebel's treatment of Trobriand law discusses both legal processes (1954: 183–186, 195–197).

2   With this variable, and with other variables also, our figures may be underestimates. They can never be overestimates, due to the nature of ethnographic literature and the strict coding procedures followed. In other words, if an ethnographer failed to record a reason for an execution, it does not appear in his or her publications; obviously, if it is not in the literature, coding procedures cannot find and retrieve the reason. On the other hand, frequencies would not be inflated unless a coder inferred the presence of a reason when none had been described.

3   John Lofland, in his study of the dramaturgy of state executions (1977), distinguishes between *open* and *concealed* executions. His distinction corresponds to the *open/closed* dimension of the typology. The *public* category of the typology is the same as Lofland's *open* execution, but the *private* and *secret* categories would both be covered by his *concealed* execution; however, his description of concealed executions, with reference to such factors as "restricted media," suggests that this type of execution in application fits the private, and not the secret, category of the typology.

4   It is interesting that Leach, a long-time critic of cross-cultural research (Leach 1950), feels competent to assert that deterrence theory is "part of the mythology of *all* legal systems." (Italics added for emphasis.) I believe that any anthropologist who is seeking universals, and this includes Leach, should be willing to conduct a small-scale, cross-cultural study that employs a probability or representative sample of societies in order to ascertain whether or not the custom, practice, or belief is found in all societies in his sample. In commenting upon Leach's review (1950) of Murdock's *Social Structure* (1949), Hendrix (1975: 136) has stated:

> Leach (1950: 108) suggested that we should ignore Murdock's data and attend only to his theorizing. The lesson to be learned is perhaps almost the opposite. We should never ignore any useful ideas, but we should be mindful of whether these ideas are supported by facts. Obviously, we should set more store by those that are than by those that are not, instead of evaluating them by use of ulterior criteria.

5   The Kurds of Iraq provide our only example of capital punishment used to wipe out an insult to honor. However, throughout the Arab Muslim Near East, intrafamily homicide for family honor occurs, and it occurs with great frequency in some regions (Kressel 1981). The wrongdoer is usually a woman who has allegedly engaged in premarital sex relations or who has been unfaithful to her husband. Stoning the woman is a common means of execution. Members of her lineage cast the first stones, and then the community participates.

CHAPTER 5

1   It is possible in very small hunting and gathering bands that generations may pass without the appearance of an individual who creates fear in others. This may be the case for the small remnant population of shellfish gatherers, recently discovered in the Philippines, who are known as the Tasaday (Nance 1975). The editors of a recent book on aggression have noted that the "Tasaday are a special case. Comprising only 26 individuals, 13 of them children, when discovered in 1966, they have not been well studied" (Goldstein and Segall 1983: 6).

2   If the spirits of the dead could harm the living, capital punishment would not be a final solution; that is, a community might not execute a wrongdoer, say a killer or a sorcerer, if they thought he might give them more problems as a malevolent spirit. Examples of such forebearance were not found, however. What was found is evidence that precautions are taken to prevent spirits from causing problems; e.g., the king of the Ganda ". . . was afraid that if he did not honor the dead chief [whom he had ordered executed] the ghost would haunt him" (Kagwa 1934: 87).

CHAPTER 6

1   Not only does Hoebel quote the passage almost in its entirety but a recent article in the *Journal of Anthropological Research* (Dillon 1980b: 437) quotes the complete text.

2   The Associated Press reported on September 2, 1982, that federal authorities had ended their investigation of the killing of Ken McElroy, and that they would not return any indictments. The U.S. Attorney in charge said that a suspect was identified in the investigation, but he refused to say whether or not it was the man named by McElroy's widow (*New York Times,* September 3, 1982, A-10).

CHAPTER 7

1   The Yanamamö (Yanoama) are a sample society that was classified as "Feud, no council." Becher (1960), not Chagnon, was the author of the ethnography in the PSF. (Chagnon uses the spelling Yanamamö, the HRAF Files, following Becher use the spelling Yanoama for the same group.) The Chagnon example was found after coding and data analysis had been completed. When Chagnon's description was coded and compared with the codes derived from Becher's data, additional codes were found. From the Chagnon example, the codes are: sexual offense, no judicial torture, political leader decides, political leader executes, no *supplice*, weapons used, and reason—disposal of wrongdoer. From Becher's data, the sexual offense was incest, not adultery.

2   The Huron Indians of North America, a matrilineal people without fraternal interest groups but with councils of chiefs at the village, tribe, and confederacy levels of sociopolitical organization, illustrate the greater ease with which political leaders can punish wrongdoers in such societies. The Huron are culturally very similar to one of the sample societies—the Iroquois. Among the Huron, clan segments, villages, and tribes were responsible for the behavior of their members. Thus they brought pressure to bear on an individual to behave properly. If social pressure failed, the wrongdoer might be killed. "One woman is reported to have been killed by her brother because she was an incorrigible thief" (Trigger 1969: 80). Expulsion from their longhouses was another possible punishment among the Huron (Trigger 1969: 80–81). If the offense was witchcraft or treason, Huron chiefs were likely to meet in secret, and, if the culprit was judged guilty, an "executioner was appointed to kill him without warning." On occasion, however, a trial took place. Torture was sometimes used to make the witch reveal the names of accomplices. Then followed further torturing with fire. The head was split open and the body burned. A specific case is described in primary materials from the early 1600s (Thwaites 1896–1901, 14: 37–39). Witches were so feared that anyone had the right to kill a witch; however, most people refrained from doing so, in order to avoid being accused of murdering an innocent person. Thus, the task of disposing of witches was normally left to the chiefs (Trigger 1969: 88–89).

3   The only monograph-length treatment of fraternal interest group theory is to be found in a cross-cultural study of reproductive rituals by Paige and Paige (1981). Their major hypothesis is that uncentralized political systems with fraternal interest groups are more likely to have reproductive rituals than political systems without fraternal interest groups. The political behavior of such groups is responsible for the rituals. Considerable support can be found for this theory. (For a lengthy review of the study, see McElroy 1982.) The sample societies used in the study are bands and tribes, which do not have central governments with independent military organizations. These societies are classified as having either strong or weak fraternal interest groups.

The theory set forth by Paige and Paige takes a different view of tribal society than does confrontation theory; for the former theory, tribes have no government, and fraternal interest groups are either strong or weak. Confrontation theory, on the other hand, posits the existence of government (e.g., political leaders and/or councils) in tribal society and considers the relative strength of competing fraternal interest groups within these societies.

CHAPTER 8

1   The Issawi translation has been used in preference to other available translations, since Charles Issawi's mode of expression more nearly approximates that of modern social science writers.

2   The concept of a "mature" state has been taken from Claessen and Skalnik, *The Early State* (1978). Although this lengthy volume focuses almost solely upon the early state and its several forms (inchoate, typical, and transitional), it does provide a brief look at the type of state that follows developmentally the early state (1978: 22, 23, 588, 605). The mature state has an administrative apparatus that is dominated by appointed officials; kinship influences are only marginal aspects of government; and private property prevails in the means of production (as a market economy and overtly antagonistic classes develop).

The concept of despotic state has been used, instead of early state, because the focus of this study has been upon capital punishment—its extent and the manner in which it is employed. In other words, the emphasis of the research in this chapter has been to explain the presence of cruel forms of the death penalty in some states, rather than to explain the development of statehood.

3   Some consistency can be found between this coding and Spitzer's coding of societies into four punishment types. Four of the despotic states were coded by Spitzer (1975: 620–621) as Punishment Type I, his Type I being the severe end of his continuum. One despotic state was coded by Spitzer as Type III. Only one of Claessen's early states is included in this study—the Azande, coded here as a despotic state and by Claessen as an

inchoate early state (1978: 593). Less consistency is found between the coding and Cohen's classification into incorporative states and expropriated states. Two of the despotic states were coded by Cohen (1969: 663) as incorporative states, but one of the mature states was also coded as an incorporative state; two of the despotic states were coded as expropriated states. This lack of perfect consistency may in part stem from different defining criteria and also from Cohen's failure in the data table to distinguish between inchoate and successful incorporative states.

4   In a cross-cultural study of warfare, using a sample of fifty societies, Otterbein (1970/85: 136) found only 6 chiefdoms.

5   The presence of at least one of these two forms of torture was used as the basis for classifying seven states as despotic; although technically torture should not be given as a prediction, it seems appropriate to include torture here along with the predictions for the sake of completeness.

6   Included in this list of predictions are the characteristics used to classify five states as mature; they are included here for the sake of completeness.

CHAPTER 9

1   A self-inflicted execution—or judicial suicide, as I am calling it—is uncommon (only 5 cases) and confined to the more complex political systems. Perhaps the most famous example of judicial suicide, both in social science and in popular literature, is the Japanese custom of *seppuku* or *harakiri*—ceremonial suicide by disembowelment (Benedict 1946a: 166–168, 199–205; Lebra 1976: 190–200; Clavell 1975). The use of *seppuku* as a penalty, as opposed to its use as a voluntary death, is explained by Lebra as a privilege, restricted to the samurai class, that "saved the offender from the disgrace of being put to death by an executioner. *Seppuku* is thus associated with the honor of the ruling class . . . of feudal Japan" (1976: 191). Lebra's explanation for Japan seems also to hold for the Ashanti, the only state-level society in the sample with judicial suicide. The characteristics of a state-level society with judicial suicide, thus, are that it is a socially stratified society; that the practice is restricted to members of the upper class; and that suicide is considered an honorable way to die, in that it prevents someone of lower status from executing the condemned.

However, these characteristics do not apply to the nonstate, but relatively complex, societies in the sample that also have judicial suicide. Of these cultures, the Trobriand Islanders, who jump to their deaths from coconut palm trees, provide the best-known example (see Chapter 4, pp. 24–25). In this case, public censure and the individual's feelings of shame are important characteristics. However, in another well-described, but not well-known, example—Tikopia—the chief forces the condemned man to go to sea. Tradition tells him that he is supposed to sink the canoe, once he has lost sight of land. Because the condemned man is supposed to knock the bottom out of the boat—an act of suicide—the case was not classified as death by exposure or exile. (See Chapter 1, pp. 5-6, for a case in which the man chose not to do this, but attempted instead to escape.) The characteristics of middle-level societies with judicial suicide, thus, are broad in nature: The political leader or the community brings against the offender an action that can range anywhere from ostracism to the use of force. If there is a cultural norm that defines suicide as appropriate behavior, and if the offender feels humiliated, he may commit suicide (e.g., Trobriand Islands). If he does not feel humiliated, he may attempt to escape (e.g., Tikopia).

References

Arendt, Hannah
1963 Eichmann in Jerusalem: A Report on the Banality of Evil. New York, Penguin Books.

Becher, Hans
1960 Die Surára und Pakidái: Zwei Yanonami-Stamme in Nordwest-brasilien. (HRAF translation.) Hamburg, Museum für Völkerkunde, Mittheilungen, 26: 1–133.

Bedau, Hugo Adam
1979 The Death Penalty in the United States: Imposed Law and the Role of Moral Elites. *In* The Imposition of Law, edited by S. B. Burman and B. E. Harrell-Bond. New York, Academic Press, pp. 45–68.

Benedict, Ruth
1946a The Chrysanthemum and the Sword: Patterns of Japanese Culture. Boston, Houghton Mifflin.

1946b Patterns of Culture. New York, New American Library, a Mentor Book. (Originally published in 1934.)

Boas, Franz
1888 The Central Eskimo. Bureau of American Ethnology, Annual Report 6: 399–699. Washington, D.C., Smithsonian Institution.

1947 Anthropology. *In* Encyclopedia of the Social Sciences. New York, Macmillan, 2: 73–110. (Originally published in 1930.)

1965 The Mind of Primitive Man. New York, Free Press. (Originally published in 1938.)

Boehm, Christopher
  1984   Blood Revenge: The Anthropology of Feuding in Montenegro
         and Other Tribal Societies. Lawrence, University of Kansas Press.

  1985   Execution within the Clan as an Extreme Form of Ostracism.
         Social Science Information, 24(2): 309–321.

Boyer, Paul, and Stephen Nissenbaum
  1974   Salem Possessed: The Social Origins of Witchcraft. Cambridge,
         Harvard University Press.

Carniero, Robert L.
  1981   The Chiefdom: Precursor of the State. *In* The Transition to
         Statehood in the New World, edited by G. D. Jones and R. R. Kautz,
         Cambridge, Cambridge University Press, pp. 37–79.

CBS News
  1982   Bully. Produced by Suzanne St. Pierre, for "60 Minutes."
         Broadcast January 31 and May 23.

Chagnon, Napoleon A.
  1979   Is Reproductive Success Equal in Egalitarian Societies? *In*
         Evolutionary Biology and Human Social Behavior: An Anthropological
         Perspective, edited by N. A. Chagnon and William Irons. North
         Scituate, Mass., Duxbury Press, pp. 374–401.

Churchill, Winston S.
  1956   A History of the English-Speaking Peoples. Vol. 1, The Birth of
         Britain. New York, Dodd, Mead.

Claessen, Henri J. M.
  1978   The Early State: A Structural Approach. *In* The Early State, edited
         by Henri J. M. Claessen and Peter Skalnik. The Hague, Mouton, pp.
         533–596.

  1979   The Balance of Power in Primitive States. *In* Political Anthropol-
         ogy: The State of the Art, edited by S. Lee Seaton and Henri J. M.
         Claessen. The Hague, Mouton, pp. 183–195.

Claessen, Henri J. M., and Peter Skalnik, eds.
  1978   The Early State. The Hague, Mouton.

Clavell, James
  1975   Shogun: A Novel of Japan. New York, Atheneum.

Clinard, Marshall B.
  1978   Cities with Little Crime: The Case of Switzerland. Cambridge,
         Cambridge University Press.

Cohen, Yehudi A.
1969   Ends and Means in Political Control: State Organization and the Punishment of Adultery, Incest, and Violation of Celibacy. American Anthropologist 71: 658–687.

Colbacchini, Antonio, and Cesar Albisetti
1942   Os Boróros Orientais Orarimogodógue do Planalto Oriental de Mato Grosso. (HRAF translation.) Brasiliana, Grande Formato, Serie 5a, vol. 4. São Paulo, Companhia Editora Nacional.

Davis, James Allan
1980   General Social Surveys, 1972–1980: Cumulative Codebook. Chicago, National Opinion Research Center.

Dillon, Richard G.
1980a   Violent Conflict in Metá Society. American Ethnologist 7: 658–673.

1980b   Capital Punishment in Egalitarian Society: The Metá Case. Journal of Anthropological Research 36: 437–452.

Durkheim, Émile
1973   Two Laws of Penal Evolution. Translated from the 1899 edition by T. Anthony Jones and Andrew T. Scull. Economy and Society 2: 278–308. (Translator's Introduction, pp. 278–284.)

Durkheim, Émile, and Marcel Mauss
1963   Primitive Classification. Translated from the French edition (1903) and edited with an introduction by Rodney Needham. Chicago, University of Chicago Press.

Foucault, Michel
1977   Discipline and Punish: The Birth of the Prison. New York, Pantheon Books.

Goldstein, Arnold P., and Marshall H. Segall, eds.
1983   Aggression in Global Perspective. New York, Pergamon Press.

Goodenough, Ward H.
1980   Some Reflections on the Common Denominator of Cultures. Society for Cross-Cultural Research Newsletter 8 (1): 10–17.

Grinnell, George B.
1923   The Cheyenne Indians: Their History and Ways of Life. 2 vols. New Haven, Yale University Press.

Harris, Marvin
1974   Cows, Pigs, Wars, and Witches: The Riddles of Culture. New York, Random House, Vintage Books.

Hay, Douglas
    1975   Property, Authority and the Criminal Law. *In* Albion's Fatal Tree:
            Crime and Society in Eighteenth-Century England, edited by Douglas
            Hay et al. New York, Pantheon Books, pp. 17–63.

Heizer, Robert F.
    1955   Executions by Stoning among the Sierra Miwok and Northern
            Paiute. Kroeber Anthropological Society, Papers, 12: 45–50.

Hendrix, Lewellyn
    1975   Nuclear Family Universals: Fact and Faith in the Acceptance of an
            Idea. Journal of Comparative Family Studies 6: 125–138.

Hoebel, E. Adamson
    1954   The Law of Primitive Man: A Study in Comparative Legal
            Dynamics. Cambridge, Harvard University Press.

Ibn Khaldūn
    1950   An Arab Philosophy of History: Selections from the Prolegomena
            of Ibn Khaldūn of Tunis (1332–1406). Translated and arranged by
            Charles Issawi. London, John Murray.

Inverarity, James M., and Pat Lauderdale
    1983   Sociological Analyses of the Criminal Sanction. *In* Law and
            Society: Sociological Perspectives on Criminal Law, edited by James
            M. Inverarity and Pat Lauderdale. Boston, Little Brown. pp. 285–314.

Kadish, Sanford H., and M. G. Paulsen
    1975   Criminal Law and Its Processes: Cases and Materials. 3d ed.
            Boston, Little, Brown.

Kagwa, Apolo
    1934   The Customs of the Baganda. Translated by Ernest B. Kalibala,
            edited by Max Mandelbaum. New York, Columbia University Press.

Kressel, Gideon M.
    1981   Sororicide/Filiacide: Homicide for Family Honour. Current
            Anthropology 22: 141–158.

Kurtz, Donald V.
    1978   The Legitimation of the Aztec State. *In* The Early State, edited by
            Henri J. M. Claessen and Peter Skalnik. The Hague, Mouton pp. 169–
            189.

Legacé, Robert O.
    1973   HRRF Study Guide: The Nature and Use of the Human
            Relations Resource Files. Ann Arbor, Xerox University Microfilms.

    1979   The HRAF Probability Sample: Retrospect and Prospect. Behav-
            ior Science Research 14: 211–229.

Lagacé Robert O., ed.
1977   Sixty Cultures: A Guide to the HRAF Probability Sample Files (Part A). New Haven, Human Relations Area Files.

Leach, Edmund
1950   Review of Social Structure by G. P. Murdock. Man 50 (August): 107–108.

1977   Custom, Law, and Terrorist Violence. Edinburgh, Edinburgh University Press.

Lebra, Takie Sugiyama
1976   Japanese Patterns of Behavior. Honolulu, University Press of Hawaii.

Lee, Richard B.
1984   The Dobe !Kung. New York, Holt, Rinehart and Winston.

Llewellyn, Karl N., and E. Adamson Hoebel
1941   The Cheyenne Way: Conflict and Case Law in Primitive Jurisprudence. Norman, University of Oklahoma Press.

Lofland, John
1977   The Dramaturgy of State Executions. *In* State Executions: Viewed Historically and Sociologically, edited by Horace Bleackley and John Lofland. Montclair, N.J., Patterson Smith, pp. 273–325.

Lowie, Robert H.
1946   The Bororo. *In* Handbook of South American Indians, edited by Julian H. Steward. Washington, D.C., Bulletin of the Bureau of American Ethnology, no. 143, 1: 419–434.

McElroy, Ann
1982   Ritual as Puffery/Empiricism as Defense. Reviews in Anthropology 9: 251–267.

Mackey, Philip E.
1982   Hanging in the Balance: The Anti-Capital Punishment Movement in New York State, 1776–1861. New York, Garland Publishing.

Malinowski, Bronislaw
1921   The Primitive Economics of the Trobriand Islanders. Economic Journal 31: 1–16.

1922   Argonauts of the Western Pacific. London, George Routledge and Sons.

1926   Crime and Custom in Savage Society. New York, Harcourt, Brace.

1929   The Sexual Life of Savages in Northwestern Melanesia. New York, Horace Liveright.

1939   The Group and Individual in Functional Analysis. American Journal of Sociology 44: 938–964.

1944   A Scientific Theory of Culture and Other Essays. Chapel Hill, University of North Carolina Press.

Man, Edward H.
1932   On the Aboriginal Inhabitants of the Andaman Islands. London, Royal Anthropological Institute of Great Britain and Ireland. (Originally published in 1882.)

Maxwell, Eleanor K., and Robert J. Maxwell
1980   Search and Research in Ethnology: Continuous Comparative Analysis. Behavior Science Research 15: 219–243.

Miller, Alan V.
1980   Capital Punishment as a Deterrent: A Selected Bibliography. P-452 and P-592. Monticello, Ill., Vance Bibliographies.

Moore, Sally Falk
1978   Law as Process: An Anthropological Approach. London, Routledge and Kegan Paul.

Morris, Richard B.
1976   Encyclopedia of American History: Bicentennial Edition. New York, Harper and Row.

Murdock, George P.
1934   The Ganda of Uganda. In his Our Primitive Contemporaries. New York, Macmillan, pp. 508–550.

1945   The Common Denominator of Cultures. In The Science of Man in the World Crisis, edited by Ralph Linton. New York, Columbia University Press, pp. 123–142.

1949   Social Structure. New York, Macmillan.

1965   Anthropology and Its Contribution to Public Health. In his Culture and Society: Twenty-four Essays. Pittsburgh, University of Pittsburgh Press, pp. 49–57. (Originally published in 1952.)

1967   Ethnographic Atlas. Pittsburgh, University of Pittsburgh Press.

1975   Outline of World Cultures, 5th ed. New Haven, Human Relations Area Files.

Murdock, George P., et al.
   1982   Outline of Cultural Materials. 5th rev. ed. New Haven, Human
   Relations Area Files.

Nance, John
   1975   The Gentle Tasaday: A Stone Age People in the Philippine Rain
   Forest. New York, Harcourt Brace Jovanovich.

Naroll, Raoul
   1964   On Ethnic Unit Classification. Current Anthropology 5: 283–312.

Naroll, Raoul, Gary L. Michik, and Frada Naroll
   1976   Worldwide Theory Testing. New Haven, Human Relations Area
   Files.

New York Times
   1982   U.S. Ends Investigation of Town Bully's Slaying. Sept. 3, p. A–10.

Otterbein, Keith F.
   1967   Mortuary Practices in Northeastern Nigeria. Bulletin of the
   Cultural Research Institute, Government of India 6 (1&2): 10–19.

   1968a   Cross-Cultural Studies of Armed Combat. Studies in International Conflict, Research Monograph No. 1, Buffalo Studies 4(1): 91–
   109.

   1968b   Higi Armed Combat. Southwestern Journal of Anthropology
   24: 195–213.

   1968c   Internal War: A Cross-Cultural Study. American Anthropologist
   70: 277–289.

   1969a   Basic Steps in Conducting a Cross-Cultural Study. Behavior
   Science Notes 4: 221–36.

   1969b   Higi Marriage System. Bulletin of the Cultural Research Institute,
   Government of India 8 (1&2): 16–20.

   1970/85   The Evolution of War: A Cross-Cultural Study. New Haven,
   HRAF Press. (Second Edition 1985)

   1973   The Anthropology of War. In Handbook of Social and Cultural
   Anthropology, edited by J. J. Honigmann, pp. 923–958. Chicago,
   Rand McNally.

   1976   Samples and Sampling in Cross-Cultural Studies. Behavior
   Science Research 11: 107–121.

   1977   Comparative Cultural Analysis: An Introduction to Anthropology.
   2d ed. New York, Holt, Rinehart and Winston.

1979   A Cross-Cultural Study of Rape. Aggressive Behavior 5: 425–435.

1985   Feuding—Dispute Resolution or Dispute Continuation? Reviews in Anthropology 12: 73–83.

Otterbein, Keith F., and Charlotte Swanson Otterbein
1965   An Eye for an Eye, A Tooth for a Tooth: A Cross-Cultural Study of Feuding. American Anthropologist 67: 1470–1482.

Oxford English Dictionary
1971   The Compact Edition of the Oxford English Dictionary. Complete Text Reproduced Micrographically. Vols. 1 and 2. New York, Oxford University Press.

Packer, Herbert L.
1968   The Limits of the Criminal Sanction. Stanford, Stanford University Press.

Paige, Karen Ericksen, and Jeffrey M. Paige
1981   The Politics of Reproductive Ritual. Berkeley, University of California Press.

Radcliffe-Brown, Alfred R.
1964   The Andaman Islanders. Glencoe Ill., Free Press. (Originally published in 1922.)

Reese, Michael, and Sylvester Monroe
1981   Murder of a Town Bully. Newsweek, August 3, 1981, p. 33.

Rivers, William H. R.
1914   Tikopia. In his The History of Melanesian Society. Cambridge, Cambridge University Press, 1: 298–362.

Roscoe, John
1911   The Baganda: An Account of Their Native Customs and Beliefs. London, Macmillan.

Schwartz, Richard D.
1979   The Supreme Court and Capital Punishment: A Quest for Balance between Legal and Societal Morality. Law and Policy Quarterly 1: 285–335.

1980   Mores and the Law: Taking Sumner Seriously. Behavior Science Research 15: 159–180.

Schwarzschild, Henry
1982   No Matter What the Method, Execution Remains a Homicide. Special Feature, Buffalo News, December 30, 1982.

Sellin, Thorsten
  1980   The Penalty of Death. Beverly Hills, Cal., Sage Publications.

Service, Elman R.
  1962   Primitive Social Organization: An Evolutionary Perspective.
  New York, Random House.

Sheils, Dean
  1980   A Comparative Study of Human Sacrifice. Behavior Science
  Research 15: 245–262.

Slobodin, Richard
  1978   W. H. R. Rivers. New York, Columbia University Press.

Speke, John Hanning
  1864   Journal of the Discovery of the Source of the Nile. New York,
  Harper and Brothers.

Spencer, Walter B., and F. J. Gillen
  1899   The Native Tribes of Central Australia. London, Macmillan.

  1927   The Arunta: A Study of a Stone Age People. London, Macmillan.

Spitzer, Steven
  1975   Punishment and Social Organization: A Study of Durkheim's
  Theory of Penal Evolution. Law and Society Review 9: 613–637.

  1979   Notes Toward a Theory of Punishment and Social Change.
  Research in Law and Sociology 2: 207–229.

Stinchcombe, Arthur L., et al.
  1980   Crime and Punishment—Changing Attitudes in America. San
  Francisco, Cal., Jossey-Bass Publishers.

Stoner, Barbara
  1971   Why Was William Jones Killed? Bulletin, Field Museum of
  Natural History 42(8): 10–13.

Tacitus
  1872   The Works of Tacitus, vol. 2. The History, Germany, Agricola,
  and Dialogue on Orators. New York, Harper and Brothers.

Thoden van Velzen, H. U. E., and W. van Wetering
  1960   Residence, Power Groups and Intrasocietal Aggression. International Archives of Ethnography 49: 169–200.

Thwaites, Reuben G., ed.
  1896–1901   The Jesuit Relations and Allied Documents. 73 vols.
  Cleveland, Burrows.

Trigger, Bruce G.
   1969   The Huron: Farmers of the North. New York, Holt, Rinehart and
          Winston.

Turnbull, Colin M.
   1965   Wayward Servants: The Two Worlds of the African Pygmies.
          Garden City, N.Y., Natural History Press.

   1978   Death by Decree: An Anthropological Approach to Capital
          Punishment. Natural History 87(5): 50–67.

U.S. Department of Justice
   1976   Capital Punishment: 1975. National Prisoner Statistics Bulletin,
          no. SD-NPS-CP-4.

Westermeyer, Joseph
   1973   Assassination and Conflict Resolution in Laos. American Anthro-
          pologist 75: 123–131.

White, Leslie A.
   1949   The Definition and Prohibition of Incest. *In his* The Science of
          Culture. New York, Ferrar, Straus, pp. 303–329.

   1975   The Concept of Cultural Systems: A Key to Understanding
          Tribes and Nations. New York, Columbia University Press.

Wilson, Edward O.
   1975   Sociobiology: The New Synthesis. Cambridge, Harvard University
          Press, Belknap Press.

Wissler, Clark
   1923   Man and Culture. New York, Thomas Y. Crowell.

APPENDIX A

Code Sheet and Coding

CAPITAL PUNISHMENT DATA SHEET

HPS Cultural Unit _____ OWC Code _____

Sources used _____ Time _____

Coder _____ Date _____

NOTES:

Abbreviated titles, shown in capital letters (e.g., TYPOL, TREASON), were derived for computer analyses; they are those found in Appendix B, Codes.

Numbers for codings, shown beneath abbreviated titles, correspond to numbers in Appendix B.

NAME — Name of society as used by the Human Relations Area Files (HRAF)

OWC — Code for society used in the Outline of World Cultures (OWC)

TYPOL — Typology coding of societies

> 1—Mature state
> 2—Dependent native peoples
> 3—Despotic state
> 4—Chiefdom
> 5—Council, feuding not present
> 6—Council, feuding present
> 7—No council, feuding present
> 8—Bands

1. For what crimes is capital punishment used?

    TREASON — Treason

       1—No
       2—Yes

    ASSASSIN — Political assassination

       1—No
       2—Yes

    HOMICIDE — Homicide (physical assault)

       1—No
       2—Yes

    STEALING — Stealing, burglary, and robbery

       1—No
       2—Yes

    WITCHCR — Sacrilegious acts (witchcraft)

       1—No
       2—Yes

    SEXUAL — Sexual offenses

       1—No
       2—Yes

    DESERTN — Desertion in war

       1—No
       2—Yes

    OTHERCR — Other crimes

       1—No
       2—Yes

    NCRIMES — Total number of crimes for which capital punishment
                 is used

       1—One crime
       2—Two crimes
       etc.

2. Are there facilities for holding prisoners?

    PRISONS

       1—No facilities for holding prisoners
       2—Temporary incarceration
       3—Permanent incarceration (jails)
       0—No data

3. Is "judicial torture" used to obtain confessions?

    JUDICTOR

      1—No
      2—Yes
      0—No data

4. Who decides that the wrongdoer is to be executed?

    POLITLDR — Political leader (or political leader for any hierarchical
              level)

      1—No
      2—Yes
      0—No data

    COUNCIL — A council (a deliberating body of important adults)

      1—No
      2—Yes
      0—No data

    KINGROUP — His kin group

      1—No
      2—Yes
      0—No data

    RELIGPR — Religious practitioner(s)

      1—No
      2—Yes
      0—No data

    VICTKIN — Kin of victim

      1—No
      2—Yes
      0—No data

    COMMUNTY — Community

      1—No
      2—Yes
      0—No data

5. What is the social context in which the execution takes place?

    SCONTEXT

        1—Public
        2—Private
        3—Secret
        4—Both 1 and 3, above
        0—No data

6. Who is the executioner?

POLITEX — Political leader or agent of leader (could be self-appointed)

   1—No
   2—Yes
   0—No data

KINVICT — Kin of victim

   1—No
   2—Yes
   0—No data

KINOFFEN — Kin of offender

   1—No
   2—Yes
   0—No data

SELFINFL — Self-inflicted (judicial suicide)

   1—No
   2—Yes
   0—No data

COMMTYEX — Community

   1—No
   2—Yes
   0—No data

7. Does capital punishment deliberately incorporate elements of painful torture?

TORTURE

   1—No–it is simply a withdrawal of the right to live
   2—Yes (*supplice*)
   0—No data

8. What is the manner in which the death penalty is carried out?

DECAPIT — Decapitation

   1—No
   2—Yes
   0—No data

DROWNING — Drowning

   1—No
   2—Yes
   0—No data

HANGING — Hanging

    1—No
    2—Yes
    0—No data

BURNING — Burning

    1—No
    2—Yes
    0—No data

POISON — Poisoning

    1—No
    2—Yes
    0—No data

INCAPEXP — Incapacitating/exposure

    1—No
    2—Yes
    0—No data

WEAPONS — Using weapons—arrows, spears, swords, or guns

    1—No
    2—Yes
    0—No data

OTHERWAY — Other manner in which the death penalty is carried
                out

    1—No
    2—Yes
    0—No data

NWAYS — Total number of ways in which the death penalty is
         carried out

    1—One way
    2—Two ways
    etc.
    0—No data

9. What reasons are given for capital punishment by those responsible
   for the execution?

REASONS

    1—Disposal of wrongdoer
    2—Revenge—punish wrongdoer because he deserves it
    3—Set example—deterrence
    4—Other reason
    5—Both 1 and 2, above

6—Both 1 and 3, above
7—Both 3 and 4, above
0—No data

10. To what extent do the members of the political community accept capital punishment as an appropriate practice?

ACCEPTED

1—Most demand capital punishment
2—Accepted—deemed appropriate by most
3—Deemed inappropriate by most (50% or more)
4—Strongly resented by most
5—Both 1 and 3, above
0—No data

REGION — Regional code, based on first letter of OWC code

1—N, North America
2—S, South America
3—F, Africa
4—M, Mediterranean
5—E, Europe
6—R, Russia
7—A, Asia
8—O, Oceania

HRAF Probability Sample, Sources, and Codes[1]

SOCIETY LABEL	OWC[2]	EA[2]	DESCRIPTION
Amhara	MP5	Ca7	The Amhara are an agricultural people speaking a Semitic language who live on the central plateau of Ethiopia.
Andamans	AZ2	Eh1	The Andamanese are a hunting and gathering people speaking an isolated language who live on the Andaman Islands in the eastern part of the Bay of Bengal in the Indian Ocean.
Aranda	OI8	Id1	The Aranda are a hunting and gathering people speaking an Australian language who live in the Central Desert of Australia in the vicinity of Alice Springs.
Ashanti	FE12	Af3	The Ashanti are an agricultural people speaking a Twi language who live in southern Ghana in West Africa.
Azande	FO7	Ai3	The Azande are an agricultural people speaking a Niger-Congo language who live mainly in the Bahr el Ghazal province of western Sudan, with some also living in the neighboring parts of Congo-Kinshasa and the Central African Republic.
Bahia Brazilians	SO11	Cf4	The Bahia Brazilians are an agricultural people speaking Brazilian Portuguese who live in the state of Baia in northeastern Brazil, particularly in the city of Salvador (Bahia) and the surrounding Reconcàvo district.
Bemba	FQ5	Ac3	The Bemba are an agricultural people speaking a Bantu language who live in northern Zambia in Central Africa.
Blackfoot	NF6	Ne12	The Blackfoot are a hunting people speaking an Algonquian language who live on the northern Great Plains of North America in southern Alberta and northern Montana.
Bororo	SP8	Si1	The Bororo are a horticultural people speaking a Gê language who live in the Central Brazilian province of Mato Grosso.

Bush Negroes	SR8	Sc6	The Bush Negroes are a group of horticultural peoples speaking languages based on a mixture of African and European languages who live in Surinam, French Guiana, and Guyana.
Cagaba	SC7	Sb2	The Cagaba are a group of agricultural people speaking Chibchan languages who live on the Sierra Nevada de Santa Marta of northern Colombia and its environs.
Chukchee	RY2	Ec3	The Chukchee are a people speaking a Paleo-Siberian language who live in northeastern Siberia, principally on the Chukotsk Peninsula.
Cuna	SB5	Sa1	The Cuna are a horticultural and fishing people speaking a Chibchan language who live on the San Blas Islands of Panama and the neighboring coast.
Dogon	FA16	Ag3	The Dogon are an agricultural people speaking a Voltaic language who live in the Bandiagara administrative district of Mali, West Africa.
Ganda	FK7	Ad7	The Ganda are an agricultural people speaking a Bantu language who are a major population unit in Uganda in East Africa.
Garo	AR5	Ei1	The Garo are a horticultural people speaking a Tibeto-Burman language who live principally in the Garo Hills district of the state of Assam in northeastern India.
Guarani	SM4	Si10	The Guarani are an agricultural people speaking a Tupi-Guarani language who live in various local groups over a large area in southern Brazil, Paraguay, Uruguay, and Argentina.
Hausa	MS12	Cb26	The Hausa are an agricultural people speaking a Chadic language who live in northern Nigeria and southern Niger.
Hopi	NT9	Nh18	The Hopi are an agricultural people speaking a Shoshonean language who live in northeastern Arizona in the southwestern United States.
Iban	OC6	Ib1	The Iban are a horticultural people speaking a Malayo-Polynesian language who live in Sarawak, East Malaysia.

SOCIETY LABEL	OWC	EA	DESCRIPTION
Ifugao	OA19	Ia3	The Ifugao are an agricultural people speaking a Malayo-Polynesian language who live in northern Luzon in the Philippine Islands.
Iroquois	NM9	Ng10	The Iroquois are a confederacy of agricultural peoples speaking Iroquoian languages who live principally in northern New York State and in southern Ontario, Canada.
Kanuri	MS14	Cb19	The Kanuri are an agricultural people speaking a Central Saharan language who live in Bornu Province in northeastern Nigeria.
Kapauku	OJ29	Ie1	The Kapauku are a horticultural people speaking a Papuan language who live in the central highlands of West Irian (West New Guinea).
Khasi	AR7	Ei8	The Khasi are a horticultural people speaking a Mon-Khmer language who live in the Khasi Hills area of Assam in northeastern India.
Klamath	NR10	Nc8	The Klamath are a hunting and gathering people speaking a Lutuamian language who live in southern Oregon.
Korea	AA1	Ed1	The Koreans are an agricultural people living in the modern countries of North Korea and South Korea.
Kurd	MA11	Ci11	The Kurds are an agricultural and herding people who inhabit a large area in the modern nations of Iran, Iraq, Turkey, Syria, and the U.S.S.R. The data in the file pertain mostly to southern Kurdistan.
Lapps	EP4	Cg4	The Lapps are a reindeer-herding and fishing people speaking a Finno-Ugric language who live in northern Scandinavia.

Lau	OQ6	Ih4	The Lau Fijians are a horticultural and fishing people speaking a Malayo-Polynesian language who live in the Lau Islands of southern Fiji in the central Pacific Ocean.
Lozi	FQ9	Ab3	The Lozi are a group of agricultural peoples speaking Bantu languages who live in Barotseland in western Zambia in Central Africa.
Masai	FL12	Aj2	The Masai are a pastoral people speaking a Sudanic language who live in southern Kenya and northern Tanzania in East Africa.
Ojibwa	NG6	Nf1	The Ojibwa are a group of peoples with economies based on fishing, hunting and gathering, or horticulture who speak an Algonquian language and live in the western Great Lakes area of the United States and Canada.
Ona	SH4	Sg3	The Ona are a hunting and collecting people speaking a Chonan language who live in Tierra del Fuego at the southern tip of South America.
Pygmies	FO4	Aa5	The Mbuti Pygmies are a group of hunting and gathering peoples speaking principally Central Sudanic languages who live in the Ituri Forest of Congo-Kinshasa in Central Africa.
Santal	AW42	Ef1	The Santal are an agricultural people speaking a Munda language who live principally in West Bengal in India.
Senussi	MT9	Cd20	The Libyan Bedouin, of which the Senussi form an important religious sect, speak Arabic and live in the Libyan or Western Desert of Egypt and eastern Libya.
Serbs	EF6	Ch1	The Serbs are an agricultural people speaking a Serbo-Croatian language who live in Serbia in southern Yugoslavia.
Shluh	MW11	Cd5	The Shluh are a group of agricultural peoples speaking a Berber language who live in the High Atlas Mountains of southern Morocco.
Sinhalese	AX4	Eh6	The Sinhalese are an agricultural people speaking an Indic language who live on the island of Ceylon (Sri Lanka).

SOCIETY LABEL	OWC	EA	DESCRIPTION
Somali	MO4	Ca2	The Somali are a pastoral and agricultural people speaking a Cushitic language who live in Somalia and the Territory of the Afars and the Issas in the Horn of Africa.
Tarahumara	NU33	Ni1	The Tarahumara are an agricultural people speaking a Uto-Aztecan language who live in the mountains of the northern Mexican state of Chihuahua.
Tikopia	OT11	Ii2	The Tikopians are a horticultural people speaking a Malayo-Polynesian language who live on the island of Tikopia in the British Solomon Islands Protectorate in the South Pacific.
Tiv	FF57	Ah3	The Tiv are an agricultural people speaking a Niger-Congo language who live in Central Nigeria.
Tlingit	NA12	Nb22	The Tlingit are a fishing people speaking a Na-Dene language who live in southeastern Alaska on the North Pacific Coast of North America.
Toradja	OG11	Ic5	The Toradja are an agricultural people speaking a Malayo-Polynesian language who live in the central part of the Indonesian island of Celebes.
Trobriands	OL6	Ig2	The Trobrianders are a tropical horticultural people speaking a Malayo-Polynesian language who live in the Trobriand Islands off the eastern coast of New Guinea.
Truk	OR19	If2	The Trukese are a horticultural and fishing people speaking a Malayo-Polynesian language who live on Truk Atoll in the Eastern Caroline Islands in the Central Pacific.
Tucano	SQ19	Se12	The Tucano are a horticultural people speaking a Tucanoan language who live in northwestern Brazil and southeastern Colombia along the Rio Negro.
Tzeltal	NV9	Sa2	The Tzeltal are an agricultural people speaking a Mayan language who live in the Chiapas highlands of southern Mexico.

Wolof	MS30	Cb2	The Wolof are an agricultural people speaking a Niger-Congo language who live in the West African countries of Senegal and Gambia.
Yakut	RV2	Ec2	The Yakut are a pastoral people speaking a Turkic language who live in north-central Siberia in the Soviet Union.
Yanoama	SQ18	Sd4	The Yanoama are a group of horticultural peoples speaking an isolated language who live in the uppermost reaches of the Orinoco River in southern Venezuela and in the neighboring parts of northern Brazil.

CULTURES	HRAF NUMBERS	SOURCE NUMBERS[3] AND PAGES
Amhara	MP5	1:308,311,321,333; 4:403
Aranda	OI8	1:40,111,168,409,443–444,467
Ashanti	FE12	3:42–43,184–185,228,280,336,375, 377–378; 19:40,90; 26:130
Azande	FO7	10:246; 29:106–107; 3:32; 9:258; 28:199
Bahia Brazilians	SO11	4:284
Bemba	FQ5	3:167; 5:91; 7:85–86
Blackfoot	NF6	4:185
Bush Negroes	SR8	1:203,289; 2:38; 3:7–8,17–19; 6:224–225, 242
Cagaba	SC7	1:145,149–150; 4:199; 5:882; 7:99, 115–116,181
Chukchee	RY2	1:573–574,662–663
Cuna	SB5	2:8–9,79,96–97; 3:79; 12:142; 17:627; 33:44
Dogon	FA16	2:222
Ganda	FK7	2:129,202,261–262,264,289,622; 4:350, 358,360–361; 8:79,81–84,87,98,131,170
Garo	AR5	1:296; 2:70,74; 4:113; 6:170; 8:1045–1046, 1049
Guarani	SM4	5:92
Hausa	MS12	3:183; 4:285; 10:11; 15:94,160,338,340
Hopi	NT9	1:162,252; 3:108
Iban	OC6	2:13,75; 4:2,130; 15:30
Ifugao	OA19	2:61–85,107; 12:113
Iroquois	NM9	1:321–324; 8:32; 34:88–90,96; 41:26,85, 236
Kanuri	MS14	1:22,25,105
Kapauku	OJ29	1:32,146–157,164–174,194,244–245,269, 273,285; 5:45,106,127,209
Khasi	AR7	1:93
Klamath	NR10	1:1–2; 2:156
Korea	AA1	(Sources only) 1; 2; 4; 5; 14; 37; 48; 49; 52

CULTURES	HRAF NUMBERS	SOURCE NUMBERS[3] AND PAGES
Kurd	MA11	2:30,32,41,47,185–186; 8:11,56
Lapps	EP4	2:112,131
Lau	OQ6	1:158; 2:60,64
Lozi	FQ9	4:211,238
Masai	FL12	13:123; 18:216–217
Ojibwa	NG6	21:120,194,279,294
Ona	SH4	1:387–388,406,439,812,854,883,887, 891–892,902–905,1054–1055
Pygmies	FO4	2:186,190,231,236
Santal	AW42	2:129–130; 4:134
Senussi	MT9	1:106,181–184; 2:111,148
Serbs	EF6	4:41; 6:190; 7:39,43; 10:96; 19:129–130
Shluh	MW11	1:374; 2:282–283,318; 4:92,94
Sinhalese	AX4	8:524
Somali	MO4	1:97,107–108; 18:244,286; 21:22,39,292
Tarahumara	NU33	1:213,332; 2:325,456; 13:138–139
Tikopia	OT11	2:329; 9:112; 16:306–307,310; 19:179–180; 20:287,305–306; 24:130
Tiv	FF57	2:74–75
Tlingit	NA12	1:200; 4:145–155; 18:39,129
Toradja	OG11	1:7,38,42; 2:16,77,85,213–214,218–219, 232,441
Trobriands	OL6	1:64–65; 4:77–80,117–118; 5:447; 8:10
Truk	OR19	1:120,142,145,151; 22:114; 24:11,254,271, 394
Tucano	SQ19	4:269,353,466; 5:155–161,269
Tzeltal	NV9	3:456–457,462–463,468; 7:76,240,278
Wolof	MS30	1:59
Yakut	RV2	2:134; 7:224
Yanoama	SQ18	2:72

NAME	OWC	TYPOL	TREASON	ASSASSIN	HOMICIDE	STEALING	WITCHCR	SEXUAL	DESERTN	OTHERCR	NCRIMES	PRISONS	JUDICTOR	POLITLDR	COUNCIL	KINGROUP	RELIGPR	VICTKIN	COMMUNTY	SCONTEXT	POLITEX	KINVICT	KINOFFEN	SELFINFL	COMMTYEX	TORTURE	DECAPIT	DROWNING	HANGING	BURNING	POISON	INCAPEXP	WEAPONS	OTHERWAY	NWAYS	REASONS	ACCEPTED	REGION
AMHARA	MP5	1	1	1	2	2	2	1	1	2	4	3	0	2	2	1	1	1	1	1	2	2	1	1	1	0	0	1	2	2	1	1	1	1	2	0	0	4
ARANDA	OI8	8	1	1	2	2	2	2	1	2	3	0	1	1	1	2	1	1	1	3	1	1	1	1	1	1	1	1	1	1	1	1	2	1	1	2	2	8
ASHANTI	FE12	3	3	2	2	2	2	2	1	2	6	0	0	2	1	1	1	1	1	1	3	2	1	2	1	2	2	2	2	2	1	1	2	1	3	6	0	3
AZANDE	FO7	3	2	1	2	1	2	2	1	1	5	0	0	1	1	1	1	1	1	2	1	2	1	1	0	1	1	1	1	1	1	1	2	2	6	7	3	3
BAHIA BR	SO11	2	1	1	1	2	1	1	1	2	1	0	0	2	2	1	1	1	1	0	0	0	0	0	0	0	0	0	0	0	0	0	2	2	0	0	0	2
BEMBA	FQ5	1	1	1	2	1	1	1	1	2	4	0	0	1	1	1	1	1	1	0	0	1	1	1	1	1	0	1	1	1	1	1	1	1	0	0	0	3
BLACKFOOT	NF6	6	1	1	1	2	2	2	1	1	1	0	2	1	2	1	1	1	1	0	1	0	0	0	1	0	1	0	0	0	0	1	0	1	1	0	0	1
BUSH NEG	SR8	5	1	1	2	2	1	1	1	2	4	2	1	1	1	1	1	1	1	0	0	1	2	1	1	1	1	2	2	2	1	0	1	0	0	0	1	1
CAGABA	SC7	5	5	1	2	2	1	2	1	1	3	1	1	2	2	1	1	1	1	3	1	1	2	1	2	1	2	1	1	1	1	1	2	2	1	1	0	2
CHUKCHEE	RY2	6	2	1	1	2	2	1	1	1	1	0	2	2	1	1	2	1	1	3	3	2	2	1	2	2	2	2	2	2	2	1	1	2	2	0	0	2
CUNA	SB5	3	1	1	1	1	1	1	1	1	8	0	2	1	1	1	1	0	1	1	2	1	1	1	2	1	1	1	1	2	1	1	1	1	1	2	2	2
DOGON	FA16	5	3	1	1	1	2	1	1	2	1	2	0	2	2	1	1	0	0	0	1	1	1	0	0	0	1	1	1	1	1	1	2	0	1	0	3
GANDA	FK7	5	2	1	1	1	1	2	1	1	8	3	2	1	1	1	1	1	1	4	2	2	2	1	2	2	2	2	2	2	2	2	2	2	2	0	2	3
GARO	AR5	2	1	1	1	1	1	2	1	1	2	3	0	0	0	0	0	1	1	0	0	1	1	0	0	0	1	2	2	2	1	2	2	2	4	2	3	7
GUARANI	SM4	7	7	1	2	1	1	1	1	1	2	0	1	2	0	0	0	1	1	1	2	1	1	1	2	1	1	1	2	2	1	1	1	1	1	0	0	1
HAUSA	MS12	3	1	2	1	2	2	1	1	2	1	0	0	0	1	0	0	0	0	0	0	2	0	1	1	2	2	2	2	2	1	0	0	8	8	7	1	2
HOPI	NT9	5	1	1	2	2	2	1	1	2	3	0	0	0	1	1	1	0	0	0	1	0	1	0	0	0	0	0	0	0	1	0	0	1	1	0	0	4
IBAN	OC6	5	1	1	1	1	1	2	1	1	1	3	2	1	2	1	2	0	0	0	0	0	1	0	1	1	1	1	1	2	0	0	0	1	0	0	1	1
IFUGAO	OA19	7	1	1	2	2	2	1	1	2	1	2	2	2	1	2	1	2	1	1	2	0	2	1	1	0	1	1	1	1	1	1	1	1	0	6	8	8
IROQUOIS	NM9	5	2	1	2	1	2	1	2	5	5	0	0	2	2	1	1	1	1	3	3	2	2	1	1	2	1	1	1	1	1	2	2	1	1	1	8	8
KANURI	MS14	1	1	2	1	2	2	2	1	1	1	2	2	2	1	2	2	1	1	1	1	1	2	1	1	1	1	1	1	1	2	1	1	1	2	8	1	1
KAPAUKU	OJ29	7	1	1	2	2	1	1	1	2	7	1	0	1	1	1	1	1	1	3	3	2	1	1	1	1	1	1	1	1	2	2	2	2	5	0	0	4
KHASI	AR7	5	1	1	2	2	2	1	1	1	3	0	0	1	2	1	1	1	1	0	0	0	1	0	0	0	1	1	1	1	2	1	1	1	0	0	7	7

Society	Code																																
KLAMATH	NR10	1	0	0	0	0	0	0	0	0	0	0	0	0	0	0	0	0	0	0	0	0	0	0	1	1	1	1	2	2	1	1	1	8
KOREA	AA1	7	0	0	5	2	2	2	2	2	1	2	2	2	1	2	1	2	4	1	1	1	2	2	3	5	2	1	1	1	1	1	1	3
KURD	MA11	4	4	0	0	1	0	0	0	0	0	0	0	1	1	1	0	2	0	1	1	2	2	0	0	3	2	2	1	1	2	2	1	2
LAPPS	EP4	5	4	4	0	0	0	0	0	0	0	0	0	0	0	0	1	0	0	0	0	0	0	0	0	3	2	1	2	1	2	2	1	8
LAU	OQ6	8	0	0	0	0	0	0	0	0	0	0	0	0	1	1	0	2	1	1	1	1	2	2	0	3	1	1	2	1	2	2	2	4
LOZI	FQ9	3	4	3	1	0	1	1	1	1	1	1	1	1	1	1	1	1	0	1	2	1	1	1	0	0	1	1	1	1	2	2	1	1
MASAI	FL12	3	2	0	0	1	0	0	0	0	0	0	0	1	2	0	2	0	0	2	1	2	1	0	0	0	3	1	1	1	2	2	1	6
OJIBWA	NG6	1	0	0	2	0	2	1	2	2	1	1	0	2	0	2	0	2	0	1	2	1	2	2	0	2	2	2	1	2	1	1	1	8
ONA	SH4	2	2	1	1	2	1	1	1	1	1	1	1	0	0	1	0	1	3	0	1	1	1	1	0	2	2	1	1	2	1	1	2	8
PYGMIES	FO4	2	1	1	1	1	1	1	1	1	1	1	1	1	1	0	1	2	3	0	1	1	1	1	1	1	1	1	2	1	2	2	1	8
SANTAL	AW42	3	2	2	1	1	2	1	1	2	1	1	1	0	0	2	0	1	4	0	1	1	2	0	1	3	3	2	1	1	1	1	1	5
SENUSSI	MT9	7	2	1	2	2	2	2	1	1	1	1	1	1	2	1	2	2	0	1	0	2	1	2	1	1	2	1	1	1	2	1	1	7
SERBS	EF6	4	1	1	3	2	2	0	1	2	2	2	2	2	1	2	1	0	1	0	0	1	2	1	1	0	4	1	1	2	1	2	1	3
SHLUH	MW11	5	1	5	1	0	0	0	0	0	0	0	0	1	2	0	2	0	0	2	0	1	1	1	0	3	1	3	1	1	1	1	1	5
SINHALESE	AX4	4	0	1	0	0	0	0	2	0	0	0	0	2	2	1	2	2	0	1	0	1	2	0	0	4	3	1	1	1	2	2	1	2
SOMALI	MO4	7	2	0	0	0	0	0	1	0	1	0	1	0	1	1	1	1	0	2	1	2	1	1	0	3	4	1	2	1	2	2	1	6
TARAHUMARA	NU33	4	2	0	0	0	0	0	0	0	0	0	1	0	1	2	2	2	1	1	2	1	2	2	0	3	3	3	1	1	2	2	1	5
TIKOPIA	OT11	1	1	2	4	0	2	1	0	1	2	1	2	1	1	1	1	1	2	1	1	1	1	1	2	0	1	1	1	1	1	1	2	5
TIV	FF57	8	2	1	0	0	1	1	0	1	0	1	0	0	1	2	1	2	1	2	1	2	1	2	1	0	3	2	2	2	2	1	1	6
TLINGIT	NA12	3	1	1	0	1	1	2	1	2	0	2	0	2	2	1	2	1	2	0	2	1	1	1	0	2	2	1	2	2	1	2	1	6
TORADJA	OG11	1	8	3	3	1	1	1	1	2	1	2	1	1	1	1	1	1	1	1	1	1	1	2	3	1	7	1	1	2	2	2	1	6
TROBRIANDS	OL6	8	2	5	3	1	2	1	1	1	1	1	1	2	1	2	1	2	2	1	1	2	1	1	1	2	1	1	1	1	1	2	1	4
TRUK	OR19	8	2	2	2	1	2	0	1	1	1	1	1	2	2	1	2	1	4	2	2	1	2	2	0	5	3	5	2	2	2	2	1	4
TUCANO	SQ19	8	1	0	1	1	1	0	1	1	1	1	1	1	1	1	1	1	0	0	1	1	1	1	1	3	5	1	1	1	1	1	2	7
TZELTAL	NV9	2	2	1	1	1	2	1	0	1	1	0	0	1	1	1	1	1	3	1	1	1	1	1	0	1	2	1	1	1	1	1	1	2
WOLOF	MS30	1	1	2	1	1	1	2	1	1	1	1	1	0	0	1	0	1	0	0	0	0	0	0	0	0	1	1	1	1	2	2	1	1
YAKUT	RV2	4	1	0	1	1	1	1	1	1	1	1	0	0	0	0	0	0	0	0	0	0	0	0	0	1	3	1	1	1	1	1	1	6
YANOAMA	SQ18	2	1	0	1	1	1	1	1	1	1	1	0	0	0	0	0	0	1	0	0	0	0	0	0	0	1	1	2	1	1	1	1	7

NOTES TO APPENDIX B

1   The list and description of societies in the HRAF Probability Sample are from
    Worldwide Theory Testing (Naroll, Michik, and Naroll 1976: Table 2, pp. 5-7).

2   **OWC** = *Outline of World Cultures*; the alphanumeric codes are used by HRAF to
    identify cultures in the HRAF Files (see Murdock 1975). **EA** = *Ethnographic Atlas*;
    the alphanumeric codes are used to identify cultures in the *Ethnographic Atlas*
    (Murdock 1967).

3   Source Numbers refer to particular ethnographic sources in the HRAF Files. All
    sources in the HRAF Probability Sample are listed by culture and number in
    Sixty Cultures (Lagacé 1977).

Index